"*Healing Racial Trauma* is outstanding. This boo[k] makeshift Band-Aids, which on the surface hid some deep-seated w... from the racial trauma I had experienced. Reading this book reminded me of the stories my Black grandparents would share of racial tension and outright hatred with my siblings and me at a very young age. Tears filled my eyes while I was holding on to every written word. I pressed beyond the immediate feelings that welled up within me to find solace and embrace authentic healing. This book is a must-read if you are serious about healing racial trauma. I give Sheila Wise Rowe a standing ovation for this life-altering book!"

Gail Dudley, author and speaker

"*Healing Racial Trauma* is one of the most revelatory, fiercely honest, and hope-filled books that I've ever read. My dear friend Sheila Wise Rowe performs open-heart surgery on those wounded by racial trauma by acknowledging their stories, validating their pain, and offering the only holistic solution: Christ-centered healing. Regardless of your ethnic background, if you read this book, you will be changed."

Dorothy Littell Greco, author of *Making Marriage Beautiful*

"*Healing Racial Trauma* is a magisterial gift for those who have suffered harm as persons of color, and it is also a revelation for those whose Whiteness has served as a pair of blinders from racial trauma. Sheila Wise Rowe brilliantly exposes, narrates, honors, and calls forth from Scripture, clients, and her own life, the stories of violation and the power of hope. There are few books I have read where I wept and raged and was humbled and offered a vision of what it might be like to fulfill the Lord's prayer: 'Thy will be done, on earth as it is in heaven.' This is a must-read for all who hunger for righteousness."

Dan B. Allender, professor of counseling psychology, founding president of The Seattle School of Theology and Psychology

"As a bicultural Indian American woman, I felt like this book was written for me. For far too long anti-Asian racism and racial trauma among Asian Americans like me have been dismissed as trivial and as not worthy of serious address. But, in Sheila Wise Rowe's *Healing Racial Trauma*, every person's story matters, and every racial wound is given equal attention. There is room here for people of every culture, ethnicity, and skin color to learn how to heal from racial trauma and navigate ongoing racism and systemic oppression in ways that can make us more resilient. I felt seen, understood, and empowered, and I know you will too."

Michelle Reyes, church planter, author, and founder-editor of the Art of Taleh website

"I hope that Black Christians, all Christians of color, and their families will use this book as an inspiration, affirmation, and a guide to addressing the bitter pieces of our stories. I expect White Christians to find a resource of patient assistance on their own road to resilience and deliverance from the vestiges of Whiteness and its demonic grip on the global household of God."

Michelle Higgins, cohost of *Truth's Table* and executive director of Faith for Justice

"With a Christian's worldview, a counselor's expertise, and a survivor's personal perspective, Sheila Wise Rowe weaves together her personal memoir with history, social science, and a biblical framework to offer a pathway for healing to those who have experienced racial trauma. She also brings a Galatians 6:2–like advocacy for all who pray for healing and restoration of our brothers and sisters."

Kristie Anyabwile, Bible teacher and author, editor of *His Testimonies, My Heritage: Women of Color on the Word of God*

"I facilitate conversations about race that often address the history and effects of racial trauma on people of color. There have been lots of books available as resources for the '101-level' conversations, but Sheila Wise Rowe has provided a much-needed resource for those who are ready to go further. As a Black woman living in the United States, *Healing Racial Trauma* is a balm to my own wounds from racial trauma. I highly recommend it to anyone seeking healing for themselves and others. I am particularly grateful that Wise Rowe expands the conversation to other groups of people of color. My hope is that this will bring about more solidarity among us, the walking wounded, so we can work together toward healing and wholeness."

Nilwona Nowlin, author and speaker

"Sheila Wise Rowe taught me much in this well-written, vulnerable, and heart-shaping book. As the pastor of Sheila's multiethnic church, I've too often wanted to rush my Black and Brown brothers and sisters to forgiveness, ignorant of the process of healing that must surround and support them. Her work here helped me understand something that hadn't clicked for far too long, and I'm grateful. Shining a light without shaming, I read this book and learned from an author who loves her readers, whoever they happen to be. I want my whole staff to read this, and I recommend that you read it too."

Adam Mabry, lead pastor of Aletheia Church, Boston, and author of *The Art of Rest: Faith to Hit Pause in a World That Never Stops*

HEALING
RACIAL
TRAUMA

THE ROAD TO RESILIENCE

SHEILA WISE ROWE

Foreword by Soong-Chan Rah

An imprint of InterVarsity Press
Downers Grove, Illinois

InterVarsity Press
P.O. Box 1400, Downers Grove, IL 60515-1426
ivpress.com
email@ivpress.com

InterVarsity Press® is the book-publishing division of InterVarsity Christian Fellowship/USA®, a
movement of students and faculty active on campus at hundreds of universities, colleges, and schools
of nursing in the United States of America, and a member movement of the International Fellowship
of Evangelical Students. For information about local and regional activities, visit intervarsity.org.

Scripture quotations, unless otherwise noted, are from the New Revised Standard Version of the Bible,
copyright 1989 by the Division of Christian Education of the National Council of the Churches of
Christ in the USA. Used by permission. All rights reserved.

While any stories in this book are true, some names and identifying information may have been
changed to protect the privacy of individuals.

Cover design and image composite: Christopher Tobias / Tobias Design, Inc.
Interior design: Daniel van Loon
Images: flower: © Hanka Steidle / Arcangel Images
        human profile with cracked surface: © Sarah Jarrett / Arcangel Images

ISBN 978-0-8308-4588-0 (print)
ISBN 978-0-8308-4387-9 (digital)

Printed in the United States of America ♾

InterVarsity Press is committed to ecological stewardship and to the conservation of natural
resources in all our operations. This book was printed using sustainably sourced paper.

Library of Congress Cataloging-in-Publication Data

A catalog record for this book is available from the Library of Congress.

P   25 24 23 22 21 20 19 18 17 16 15 14 13 12 11 10 9 8 7 6 5 4 3 2 1

Y   37 36 35 34 33 32 31 30 29 28 27 26 25 24 23 22 21 20

For my parents

Robert Wise, who gave me deep roots, and

Mae Wise, who gave me wings to fly.

CONTENTS

Foreword by Soong-Chan Rah   *ix*

1 Wounds   *1*

2 Fatigue   *21*

3 Silence   *39*

4 Rage   *54*

5 Fear   *69*

6 Lament   *85*

7 Shame   *101*

8 Addiction   *113*

9 Freedom   *125*

10 Resilience   *141*

Acknowledgments   *157*

Genogram   *159*

Group Discussion Guide   *161*

Glossary   *167*

Notes   *172*

FOREWORD

Soong-Chan Rah

Nearly two decades ago, before the topic of race and racial reconciliation became the latest fad for some believers, a small group of Christians in the Boston area gathered to envision what a conversation on race and emotional and spiritual healing could look like. It was a diverse group of pastors and leaders from three different churches representing multiple ethnic groups. The clear thought leaders of this group were my dear friends Sheila Wise Rowe and Nicholas Rowe. As we planned a conference to discuss the questions and issues around this conversation and the necessary spiritual warfare for a fruitful gathering, my admiration for this powerful ministry couple continued to grow. Over two decades of friendship, my respect for their ministry has not waned in the slightest as I have seen their integrity result in deep impact on both a local and global scale.

There was no fanfare, media coverage, or national attention on the conference we planned together. The number of participants would be considered paltry when compared to the conferences now held on this topic among evangelicals. What I remember about that gathering was the resounding spiritual impact it had on my own life. Even after many years of engaging the topic of racial reconciliation through multiple venues and contexts, key moments of that gathering still linger. I most distinctly remember Sheila

Wise Rowe standing before the gathering and offering a prayer of healing from the trauma of racial wounds. Her words were endowed with grace and filled with spiritual authority. Sheila applied all of her training as a counselor, her strength as a black woman, and her standing as a spiritual leader to bring healing to the racial trauma so endemic to our society.

The violent trauma inflicted by the diseased and dysfunctional narrative of White supremacy has often gone unaddressed in our discourse on race. We must continue to do the work of historical and social analysis that provides insight into the trauma of racism. The generational impact of America's original sin and the ongoing suffering inflicted through contemporary expressions such as mass incarceration, family separation at the border, and the rejection of refugees and asylum seekers must be examined. Theological work must also continue as we dig deeper into Scripture to discern God's words on the subject. But we may need more.

Some of our most profound social ills—and what is Making America Awful Again—is an inability to deal with the social-psychological trauma of White supremacy. Our social analysis and theological inquiry could use a good dose of pastoral psychology in order for complete healing to occur. This healing is not merely for the victim. In some ways the victimizers have also been traumatized. They have been traumatized into believing that their way is the path to greatness rather than seeking first the kingdom of God. This is a severe social-psychological illusion. Both the victims and perpetrators are susceptible to the ongoing trauma of White supremacy.

Fresh voices and perspectives are desperately needed. The cycle of evidence, denial, and amnesia cannot be broken without an intrusive event. The reality of trauma on a social-psychological level has been missed in this dialogue, and this text by Sheila Wise Rowe is the necessary antidote.

With honesty, truth, wisdom, and grace, Sheila Wise Rowe brings a fresh and distinct perspective in our conversation on race, offering heartbreaking and gut-wrenching stories that still manage to instill hope and healing. I have had the personal gift of sitting under Sheila's teaching, and now you also have that opportunity. Please embrace the opportunity to learn from this much-needed perspective. Sheila Wise Rowe's voice is a voice you want and need to hear.

CHAPTER ONE

WOUNDS

They have treated the wound of my people carelessly,
saying, "Peace, peace," when there is no peace.

JEREMIAH 6:14

We are tired of having our checks cut off without warning or investigation because of malicious gossip and lying officials! We are tired of hostile social workers and supervisors!"[1]

On the afternoon of June 2, 1967, The Mothers for Adequate Welfare, a group of poor Black and a few White mothers staged a protest at the offices of the Public Welfare Department on Blue Hill Avenue in Roxbury, Massachusetts. Hastily handwritten flyers were taped to telephone poles and shop windows inviting the community to join in the protest.

The sit-in was peaceful even after the mothers, unable to air their grievances, refused to leave. They spent the night in the foyer huddled together on the grimy linoleum floor. The next day things quickly took a turn for the worse after the mothers aired their demands but received no promise of redress. The mothers wrapped a bicycle chain around the handles of the glass double entry doors to prevent the police from entering and the staff from leaving. The police called for reinforcements. A mass of uniformed officers arrived and smashed the glass to reclaim the building.

One of the mothers shouted from an open window, "They're beating our Black sisters in here!" The police dragged the battered but still defiant mothers out of the building, down granite steps covered in blood and shards of glass, and threw them into awaiting police vans. The crowd outside erupted and rushed the police, who in turn indiscriminately clubbed and arrested people. Despite pleas for calm from local church leaders and community activists' word of honor, the unrest spread throughout the community. A riot ensued across ten blocks of Blue Hill Avenue.

For several decades Southern Black folks carrying suitcases full of prized possessions fled poverty and threats of lynching to pursue the elusive dream of a better life in Western and Northern cities like Boston. By the early 1960s, turbulence and race riots plagued much of the country yet bypassed Boston. The city had a self-congratulatory air because its predominantly African American community of Roxbury exercised restraint while other cities burned. Everything changed that humid day in June.

I was seven years old at the time. That night in my aunt and uncle's apartment, I watched the nightly news report bearing witness to mothers treated like chattel and an agitated crowd cursing and hurling rocks at the police. The reporter said the violence would likely carry on throughout the night. As we watched in stunned silence, suddenly we heard someone pounding on the front door. I hid nearby but within earshot as my uncle barked, "Who is it?" He unlatched the deadbolt, and on the other side of the door stood my dad, Robert Wise, dressed in black. His speech was halting as if he had run a road race: "We don't have to take this crap anymore. Come on; let's go beat up some Whiteys." My uncle declined, and with a dismissal of his hand my father bolted down the stairs. I spent the night listening for the front door to open or a floorboard to squeak upon Dad's return. Eventually, he made it home safely. Perhaps he shared with my mother (also known as Momae) what happened that night, but not a word was said in my presence.

The rioting carried on for three days, as over one thousand demonstrators armed with rocks, bottles, and matches clashed with police officers armed with guns and billy clubs. When the smoke cleared, Blue Hill Avenue looked like a war zone strewn with debris and charred apartment buildings and storefronts. I wondered, *Was Dad partly responsible for the devastation?* Years passed before I knew of the deferred dreams of my dad and the depth of his well of trauma, grief, and rage.

In a 1968 speech titled "The Other America," Dr. Martin Luther King Jr. pointedly remarked, "In the final analysis, a riot is the language of the unheard."[2] Dr. King's remark is as relevant today as it was back then.

The recent deaths of unarmed Black men at the hands of the police, the immigration crackdown, and the rise in White supremacists have led to protests across the country, and inner cities still burn. I believe that riots are also the language of the unhealed.

When God says, "They have treated the wound of my people carelessly, saying 'Peace, peace,' when there is no peace" (Jeremiah 6:14), he acknowledges that he sees and knows that we bear wounds that have not been taken seriously. Although there is significant research on the social, economic, and political effects of racism, little research recognizes the emotional and physical effects of racism on people of color.[3]

Proverbs 13:12 tells us: "Hope deferred makes the heart sick, but a desire fulfilled is a tree of life." In his potent poem "Harlem," written in 1951, Langston Hughes gives another view of the impact of life without hope when he asks: "What happens to a dream deferred?" Langston shows how we may watch it die, live with it as an open wound, or express it outwardly as rage.

AN INVITATION

People of color have endured traumatic histories and almost daily assaults on our dignity, and we are told to get over it. We have prayed about the racism, been in denial or acted out in anger, but we have not known how to individually or collectively pursue healing from the racial trauma.

We need healing and new ways to navigate ongoing racism, systemic oppression, and racial trauma that impairs our ability to become more resilient. Resilience is the capacity to recover quickly from difficulties or to "work through them step by step, and bounce back stronger than you were before." In relation to racism, resilience refers to the ability "to persevere and maintain a positive sense of self when faced with omnipresent racial discrimination."[4] Resilience is not an inherited trait; how we think, behave, and act can help us to grow in resilience.

In this book you will meet a few people of color along the way and read their stories of oppression, healing, and resilience. I am one of them, an African American woman, author, speaker, trauma counselor, and also a survivor. The others are not random people of color but dear friends and family members whose stories carry lessons for us all. The fact that we are a diverse group is countercultural. Historians have revealed that from the earliest days of First Nation genocide and the enslavement of Africans there has been a concerted effort to keep people of color separated and to develop a caste system of sorts. Rather than seeing the commonality that we have as people of color, we have been grading whose experience is worse. In his speech "I've Been to the Mountaintop," Dr. Martin Luther King Jr. wrote, "When Pharaoh wanted to prolong slavery, he kept the slaves fighting among themselves. Whenever the slaves got together that was the beginning of getting out of slavery. Now let us maintain unity."[5]

We begin our journey with the assurance from Matthew 1:23 that "God is with us"—Emmanuel. He comforts the broken-hearted and heals and binds up our wounds (Psalm 147:3). As you read this book, my invitation to people of color is that you might experience your own life story affirmed and acquire new solidarity with other people of color. Also that you will obtain tools to help heal your racial trauma and to persevere on the road to resilience. My invitation to White folks is to be open to however these stories may challenge you to be a better friend and ally to people of color. Perhaps you will hear echoes of your own trauma that you need to address. My hope is that this book will lead you to greater empathy and activism.

People of color know that racism and racial oppression is real. We've felt the sting of each racist incident whether it was overt or covert, intentional or unintentional. Yet we've often been unaware of the full impact of the racial trauma that remains. It's important that we clarify exactly what racism and racial trauma are and how they affect us.

TYPES OF RACISM

Racism comes in different forms; it's pervasive and involves more than just the hatred of people of color. Racism is prejudice, discrimination, antagonism, or the systematic oppression of people and communities of color. In Psalm 139 we read that all humans are "fearfully and wonderfully made." Yet racism declares the lie that one racial group is superior to all others. This myth is perpetuated by the actions or inaction of the government, churches, families of origin, the media, and viral videos. The lie is accompanied by gross generalizations and caricatures of the "other." Local and global inner cities are sometimes depicted as godless hellholes, Black women as always angry, and young men of color as suspects and predators. In the world and within the church some people

uncritically ingest these distortions, and there are dire consequences. People of color face an ongoing struggle against racism
that is interpersonal, systemic, spatial, environmental, internalized,
or that involves White privilege.

Interpersonal racism. The most commonly understood form of
racism is interpersonal racism. This involves a person demeaning
and degrading the gifts, calling, motives, and body of a person of
color. There is an underlying belief that the gross generalizations
are valid, and as a result some people have permission to participate
in or silently witness prejudice, discrimination, or racism.

My ancestors languished under the horrors of slavery and the
segregation laws in Virginia, and their lives were devastated by interpersonal and systemic racism. My great-granddaddy James Coston
also experienced interpersonal racism. Although he had limited
formal education because the Colored schools only went up to the
seventh grade, he was self-taught. Great-Granddaddy read the newspaper to stay on top of current events and engaged in lively exchanges
with Whites in front of the five-and-dime. However, the ominous
cloud of interpersonal racism hung over each encounter. Granddaddy
never knew when the precipitation would turn to sunshine or lashing
rain and thunder. The White people in the town called him Coston,
but more than he'd care to count he was called "boy" or "nigger."

Systemic racism. Systemic racism manifests institutionally or
structurally. Institutional racism is defined as "the collective failure
of an organization to provide an appropriate and professional
service to people because of their color, culture or ethnic origin."[6]
Institutional, structural, and systemic racism is perpetuated in
schools, medical facilities, housing, financial services, government,
employment, courts, law enforcement, and the military. Systemic
racism not only fails to provide equitably but has the power to
subjugate people and communities of color and actively hamper
their forward movement.

At five years old, my dad's young life was torn apart by institutional racism as tuberculosis ran through Accomack County, Virginia, and soon visited his home. There were no hospitals for Black folks; medical care consisted mostly of home remedies. Dad's childhood soon ended as he watched his paternal grandfather and uncle die and his father's health decline. After months of coughing and sweating, his dad passed away. As the number of TB cases rose in the Black community, the state finally opened a TB hospital. Before the year was over, my dad also lost his mother and baby brother. Dad and his younger brother, Edward, were taken in by Granddaddy James and Grandma Mary, their maternal grandparents, who raised the boys as their own. The trauma of losing so many family members haunted my dad.

Granddaddy James was steadfast in his belief that faith in God, education, and economic independence were keys to freedom for Blacks. Granddaddy instilled this love in his grandsons. He and his brother opened a general store in the Black community located on the outskirts of town. They purchased goods from local White suppliers, and soon the store was well-stocked and flourishing. Black folks no longer needed to go into town to shop at the White-owned stores and hurry back before the sunset curfew. My dad and his grandparents experienced institutional racism firsthand: within a year the White merchant association in the town petitioned the supplier to stop selling goods to Granddaddy, and without stock, his store closed. For the community the closing of the store had more meaning than just an economic attack on one man. It was the death of a symbol and a promise of autonomy and prosperity. But other more ominous symbols were allowed to remain.

Public space racism. For decades people of color like Granddaddy were force-fed symbols such as Confederate Civil War statues, flags, and plaques prominently and proudly displayed in town and the state capital. Sometimes, the racial terror symbol was a burning

KKK cross in a field. These symbols represent public space racism in which metacommunication, a conversation happening beneath the surface, determines who is dominant, who is worthy, and who belongs. Today, battles are occurring over removing these artifacts and placing them in museums, where they belong.

Spatial racism. Dominance is also communicated through spatial racism—spaces and structures are purposefully designed to divide or change the demographics of communities. For decades highways, railroad tracks, and inaccessible areas visibly separated the rich and poor, and White folks and people of color. Because of the recent influx of White folks returning to cities, there's been a push to remove these structures to make cities "more livable." This has disrupted some economic centers of people of color; with gentrification they've been priced out of their neighborhoods. In 1987 the removal of the elevated Orange line train in Boston resulted in fewer commuters and customers in Dudley Square, a Black hub, which caused businesses to close and folks to move away. Although Dudley Square is now experiencing a renewal, some wonder if it will ever return to what it once was.

Environmental racism. Environmental racism is a collective form of racism that affects poor communities and those of color. These communities are disproportionately exposed to air, water, and chemical pollutants and also denied the same high-quality municipal services that White communities receive. Flint, Michigan, for example, experienced a water crisis when the city switched the water source to one contaminated with lead. The switch occurred in 2014, and Flint still doesn't have 100-percent clean drinking water.

White privilege. The ancestors of people of color were resilient, and Granddaddy James was no different—he stood firm even after the sabotage of his businesses. His next enterprise was a farm that had an access road he shared with a neighboring White farmer. When the farmer discovered that the new farmer was Black, he erected posts and padlocked a chain across the road, making it impossible for Granddaddy's horse and cart to take the produce to market. This act was White privilege and entitlement in action, the unmerited benefit that White people receive, unconsciously or consciously. It is born out of a sense of higher worth, power, and the right to the best resources and rewards because of Whiteness.

In the face of incredible odds, Granddaddy took his White neighbor to court. The White farmer was stunned when the judge sided with Granddaddy and ordered him to pay a tidy sum of $500, worth about $8,000 today. However, the obstacles placed in Granddaddy's way did not stop. At harvest time he brought his farm produce to market and watched as White farmers got $5 a bushel while he was lucky to get $3.

Internalized racism. The struggles and barriers that Granddaddy faced are not unique to the United States in the 1940s. They continue to this day and have broken some people of color. They have accepted the limitations placed on them and their communities and have internalized racism, conceding defeat and hopelessness. Some have engaged in colorism with others in their same ethnic or racial group, which is the prejudice or discrimination against folks with a darker skin tone.

Defensive othering. Some people of color have internalized racism by relishing their role as the "exceptional negro" or the "model minority" stereotype of a compliant Asian person. Yet underneath the façade there is self-hatred, which sides with the oppressor and gives tacit approval to the tools of oppression. It's been noted in the journal *Sociological Perspectives* that people of color sometimes engage in defensive othering: "By demonstrating that they share the same attitudes and disdain toward co-ethnics who fit with the stereotypes, they attempt to join the dominant group."[7] In this way we also try to convince ourselves of peace, peace, when there is no peace.

FORMS OF RACIAL TRAUMA

Racial trauma is real. Every day in the United States and across the world women, men, and children of color experience racism and witness lives and livelihoods devalued or lost as if they do not matter. The result is that people of color are carrying unhealed racial trauma.

Racial trauma can be defined as the physical and psychological symptoms that people of color often experience after a stressful racist incident. These personal or vicarious incidents happen repeatedly, causing our racial trauma to accumulate, which contributes to a more insidious, chronic stress.[8] When we experience a threat, our brains are wired to prepare our bodies to fight or flight. This stress response causes our nervous system, hormones, mind, and body to be on high alert. We believe we need to take immediate action against an actual threat. However, if the risk or the traumatic stress is not dealt with, our brains and bodies don't fully stand down, and we get stuck in an endless loop. Our traumatic stress triggers a physical and emotional response that then feeds our traumatic stress.

According to the report titled The Impact of Racial Trauma on African Americans, the effects of racial trauma include fear, aggression, depression, anxiety, low self-image, shame, hypervigilance, pessimism, nightmares, difficulty concentrating, substance abuse, flashbacks, and relational dysfunction. People of color also carry unhealed racial trauma in their bodies. The physical symptoms include hyperactivity, heart disease, headaches, and poor concentration.[9]

The sin of racism affects us severely and deeply, yet we remain silent or in denial, a response we learned from our ancestors for whom silence meant survival. While we continue to suffer in silence, bearing the wounds of racial trauma exacts a toll on us. There are various ways that people of color experience racial trauma:

historical, transgenerational, personal, physical, vicariously, and through microaggression, gaslighting, and moral injury. Unpacking each of these will provide a window into how racial trauma has been transmitted in our own lives and the damage it does to our mind, body, soul, spirit, and communities.

Maybe you were raised to follow the rule that whatever happens in our house stays in our house. This message of secrets and silence was not limited to us and our household but seemed to also refer to the history of our people. That message was like yeast that spreads and now affects how we live and move and have our being.

Historical racial trauma. Historical racial trauma is shared by a group rather than an individual and spans multiple generations who carry trauma-related symptoms without having been present for the past traumatizing event.[10] Slavery and the forced removal of First Nation tribes from their land caused historical trauma that continues to impact African Americans and First Nation tribes.

Anna Piccard writes that the high rates of alcoholism, drug abuse, and suicide of First Nation tribal members are a direct consequence of the violence, mistreatment, and abuses experienced at boarding schools, where First Nation children were forcibly moved for assimilation purposes. The children lost their language and cultural identity. The long braids worn by the boys were cut, and the children were given "White" first and last names. Although many have not experienced the boarding schools firsthand, the racial trauma and "injuries inflicted at Indian boarding schools are continuous and ongoing."[11] In response to the alarmingly high number of First Nation children removed from their homes, the Indian Child Welfare Act passed in 1978 gave First Nation parents and communities the legal right to have input about their children's placement in off-reservation schools, in foster care, and in adoptive homes.

Transgenerational racial trauma. The specific experience of trauma across a specific family line is called transgenerational racial trauma. Epigenetics is the study of how the transmission of information from one *generation* to the next affects the genes of offspring without altering the primary structure of DNA. Some studies are inconclusive about whether racial trauma can be passed down genetically. But other research has shown that "our minds may forget, but our bodies don't, and deep inside of every cell a memory trace is stored of every event we ever experienced and the sensations and feelings that occurred with them."[12] Researchers are also exploring how racial trauma affects our bodies; for example, diseases such as heart disease and cancer seem to be passed down transgenerationally. The Bible speaks of spiritual strongholds that occur when particular causes or beliefs are vigorously defended or upheld, either secretly or openly. We may be particularly prone to certain strongholds because individual attitudes or actions were modeled in our families or community. Racism in all forms is a stronghold that must be broken.

Other studies show that historical and transgenerational racial trauma can be transmitted to our descendants through family dynamics, storytelling, or folklore, and can affect our emotional and physical health. We have significant ties to our ancestors: "These bonds often determine the answers to a myriad of questions such as: 'Who am I?' 'Who am I to my family?' 'Who can "we" trust' and 'who are our enemies?' 'What ties me to my family?' And, most importantly, 'of these ties, which do I reject and which do I keep?'"[13] Our connection to our ancestors is not only personal; it's also collective. Entire communities of color have endured historical racial trauma like slavery, the Japanese internment, or First Nation genocide and have collectively asked similar questions. The answers affect how our communities function even now.

Personal racial trauma. My dad experienced personal racial trauma, yet he was unaware of his need for healing. While growing up he and his brother routinely dodged rocks and screams of "nigger" as they made their trek to their Colored school. He lost his parents and brother early in his life. He witnessed how Granddaddy James's aspirations were blocked at every turn and how this affected the family financially and emotionally. All of this left an indelible mark on him. I wonder if those early experiences fueled Dad's anger and passion for justice after he joined the Navy and moved to Boston. During the height of the civil rights movement, Dad and Momae joined the Nation of Islam, an African American Muslim sect. As followers of Malcolm X, they were fully immersed in radical community activism. The aim was to empower and transform Boston's Black community by any means necessary. On February 21, 1965, Malcolm X was assassinated, and my parents were devastated and disillusioned. They left the Nation of Islam. By the summer of 1965, hoping to improve our education, they enrolled my siblings and me in Operation Exodus, a voluntary school desegregation program. We joined a small number of Black students bused to schools in White communities. The education was better, but the interpersonal racism we endured—the name-calling and questioning of our intellects—was relentless and left us traumatized. Three years later Dr. Martin Luther King Jr. was murdered, and my parents recommitted their lives to Christ. But my dad was silent about the trauma of losing his parents, his brother, and then Malcolm and Martin.

Physical trauma. Years later, in April 1976 during the school desegregation era in Boston, Black attorney Ted Landsmark came to Boston City Hall for a meeting. He was met by a group of angry young White antibusing protesters from South Boston and Charlestown. They assaulted Mr. Landsmark with fists and feet, and as he tried to run away, a protester took the staff of a giant American flag and attempted to impale him. This racist beating caused emotional and physical trauma for Mr. Landsmark.

Vicarious trauma. The assault also caused vicarious trauma for many of us who saw it on TV or in the newspaper. Vicarious trauma occurs after we hear detailed trauma stories or watch dashcam videos of what the deceased or the survivors endured. It can feel like we are actually experiencing the event. It causes stress, fear, and physical symptoms similar to post-traumatic stress. The iconic photo of the Landsmark incident, titled "The Soiling of Old Glory," won a Pulitzer Prize and symbolized the contentious history of being Black in Boston and America and our mixed feelings about the flag.

Although Barack Obama served for eight years as our nation's first Black president, recent events have further exposed the truth that the United States is not a postracial society; racism is alive and well. On the morning after the 2016 election, kids and college students went to school, and adults returned to work. Some conservative and evangelical Christian news outlets boasted; many communities of color wept. That same day someone painted a racist message in large bold letters across a sprawling wall in Durham, North Carolina: "Black lives don't matter and neither does your votes." On social media the fear and trauma of people of color were mocked, and White allies were deemed overreacting "snowflakes," an insulting term suggesting they are as fragile as a speck of snow. By the time Thanksgiving rolled around the dividing lines of hostility were drawn around dinner tables, in the classroom, and at churches and businesses across the country. For many people of color there didn't seem to be much to be thankful about. I often found myself on the verge of tears and was vicariously traumatized after each news report of another Black man gunned down. I prayed, but fear lingered around the edges. I was anxious about the safety of my Black son and husband: *What if there is a traffic stop or a case of mistaken identity?* My emotions were a crescendo of anger, denial, sadness, resignation, indifference, cynicism about reconciliation, and bone-tiredness that ebbed or flowed at the latest slight or all-out assault on other people of color and me.

Microaggressions. Sometimes it is hard to share our story because the racism appears as a vapor. This "day-to-day stress can affect mental health when a large number of minor events add up and wear down a person, thus making her or him vulnerable to poor health. In the context of racism, daily hassles are described as microaggressions."[14] Microaggression comes in the form of slights or messages communicated verbally or nonverbally. Microaggression may be unconsciousness to the perpetrator, so when the bias is exposed, it is denied, or the person of color is accused of being overly sensitive.[15] Racially insensitive remarks are made such as "you are so articulate," or nonverbal messages are sent when a security guard tails us in the mall. Regardless of whether we are a teenager in a hoodie, a member of the Senate, a janitor, a celebrity, or a PhD, at some point most of us have experienced microaggression or have been profiled. Microaggression results in racial trauma; it is a lobbed grenade that creates damage because it comes when least expected and sends a message that we are alien. Harvard University professor Henry Louis Gates experienced this when he was arrested for trying to get into his own house in tony Cambridge, Massachusetts.

Racial gaslighting. When people of color experience racism and microaggression we need others to bear witness to the fact of what happened. Racial gaslighting often happens when there is no corroboration. The term *gaslighting* is taken from the title of the 1940s film *Gaslight*, which told the story of the systematic emotional abuse of a woman by her husband. In an attempt to undermine his wife's sanity and her perception of reality, the husband lies and shames her privately and publicly. Racial gaslighting describes the ways individuals or institutions try to manipulate or question people of color's sense of reality, often to assert or maintain control, superiority, or power.

Racial gaslighting happens when a White person hears a story of racial injustice and replies that the person must have done something to deserve it (they were too angry or sensitive), concludes that the person is imagining racism and just needs to get over it, or responds with a deafening silence. A public form of racial gaslighting happens when those who have no friends of color and who have never had an honest conversation with a person of color retweet and repost things that are not true yet are uncritically accepted as fact.

MORAL INJURY

The term *moral injury* has emerged from trauma work with service women and men who participated in, witnessed, or failed to prevent acts that transgressed deeply held moral beliefs and expectations.[16] Racism and systemic oppression can cause moral injury. Moral injury can be perpetrator-based or betrayal-based. Perpetrator-based moral injury is caused when people act in a way that goes against their deepest beliefs. Betrayal-based moral injury can occur when those in power—such as the government, law enforcement, the church, and parental figures—fail to act compassionately and justly. Rita Nakashima Brock writes, "Seeing someone else violate core moral values or feeling betrayed by persons in authority can also lead to a loss of meaning and faith."[17] In the end we are left disillusioned with distortions about God and others. When people of color experience a moral injury from racism, we may become angry at the injustice and also at God for not preventing it. We may question the existence of a loving God, lose trust in him, or isolate from the Lord and others.

Moral injury also happens when White brothers and sisters in Christ unwittingly behave like the world or the abusive and gaslighting husband. Rather than exhibiting the love of Christ, they follow a culture that categorizes people; turns a blind eye to slavery, lynching, Jim Crow, and mass incarceration; and now wants to build walls to keep people of color out. When the church fails to protect the most vulnerable, moral injury occurs because we expect the church to be and do better. When this happens repeatedly, the church's failure to create bridges and denial of the reality of people of color has resulted in suspicion, anger, deep wounding, and moral injury for people of color like me.

It has been said that young kids learn about God from watching how their parental figures behave. A parent or guardian with unhealed racial trauma may have taught us lessons that damaged our early perception of God. I learned that if God was like my dad, then God was volatile, unpredictable, and would ultimately abandon me. I was left with a moral injury. I didn't trust God to be there for me when I most needed help.

THE HEALING JOURNEY BEGINS

The magnitude and impact of racism and racial trauma became more evident to me when I participated in a racial trauma conference in Alabama. Monuments, plaques, and other nods to slavery and the confederacy are displayed throughout the state capital, Montgomery. In the city center is the imposing Court Square fountain, the former location of Montgomery's slave market. A historic marker there states: "Slaves of all ages were auctioned, along with land and livestock, standing in line to be inspected. . . . In the 1850s, able field hands were brought for $1,500; skilled artisans $3,000. In 1859, the city had seven auctioneers and four slave depots."

Overlooking the city center is the recently opened National Memorial for Peace and Justice, conceived by Equal Justice Initiative's founder, lawyer and activist Bryan Stevenson. The memorial, also known as the National Lynching Memorial, is similar to the Holocaust Memorial, where the words of Deuteronomy 4:9 are prominently displayed: "But take care and watch yourselves closely, so as neither to forget the things that your eyes have seen nor to let them slip from your mind all the days of your life; make them known to your children and your children's children." The National Lynching Memorial is a sacred space of remembrance and repentance. The memorial exposes the truth that from 1877 to 1950 over four thousand African American men, women, and children were lynched, often by enraged White mobs, the KKK, and law enforcement. Inside the memorial structure suspended from the ceiling are eight hundred six-foot metal monuments, each engraved with the names of victims and the county where they were lynched. Some counties had one lynching while others had so many that the monuments were covered with names. I was overwhelmed and hoped that I would not locate Accomack County, Virginia, where my people are from. When I could no longer read the names and counties I sat in silence. I read placards along a wall that noted some of the reasons for the lynchings: A Black man scared a White girl; a Black farmer refused a White man's offering price for his cottonseed. I slowly walked outside on the grounds of the memorial where there are replicas of the monuments laid out like coffins. When I found Accomack County I was undone, stunned, and angry.

The next day I visited the Legacy Museum, located on the site of former slave-trading quarters. Down a dark corridor directly inside the museum is a startling scene. Holographic images of the enslaved kept in pens. As I approached the images, they literally spoke of their pain and horror: a grieving mom looking for her children, children separated from their mother crying, "Mama, Mama," and the sound of women wailing Negro spirituals. Further inside the museum I was overwhelmed by audio, visuals, memorabilia, and images of racism and racial trauma in shocking detail. More of my painful history laid bare: four hundred years—from slavery, Jim Crow segregation laws, mass incarceration—and the racial injustice continues. Some areas offer bits of hope: references to the civil rights movement and a room with images of freedom-fighting heroes and heroines. Some names were familiar; others were new to me. As much as I needed to see hope, I also needed to see the painful truth. I held my emotions in check, but the whole experience was too much for me. I stumbled from the museum onto the sidewalk and hunched over trying to contain my sobs. Then I began to wail. I looked up and saw a White woman, also a conference participant, whose face was wet with tears. Our eyes locked; she gently shook her head and mouthed, "I have no words."

My mind flooded with the words and stories I'd written of the different forms of racism and racial trauma. It's one thing to write about it and another to see and feel it in graphic detail displayed in one place. For people of color, those definitions are more than words—they are trauma.

As painful as my experience was, it confirmed that the stories of racial trauma and oppression of African Americans and other people of color must be shared. In each successive chapter you will read of how racial trauma affected not just my friends of color and me but also our families and communities. We each bore one or more symptoms of racial trauma: fatigue, silence, rage, fear, lament, shame, and addiction. These stories are records of our journey on the road to healing and resilience. Each of the stories and the reflection and prayer prompts at the end of every chapter can help you to identify and treat the root and symptoms of racial trauma in your life. My hope is that this book will help you to make peace with your own story and obtain a renewed hope for the future.

REFLECTION AND PRAYER PROMPTS

1. How have you experienced racism and racial trauma throughout your life and in your family?

2. Who are the safe folks who can help you to process and pray through any pain, fear, or anger that has surfaced for you?

3. To the best of your ability, complete the genogram located at the end of the book. The genogram may help you to identify racial trauma passed down from your ancestors. If you have gaps in knowledge, you may need to get the oral history from your family members.

CHAPTER TWO

FATIGUE

With a yoke on our necks we are hard driven;
we are weary, we are given no rest.

LAMENTATIONS 5:5

The summer of 2014 we flew thousands of miles from Johannesburg, South Africa, to bring our son, Jonathan, back home to Boston to begin his freshman year of college. We were apprehensive about leaving him because of the US news reports of increasing racial tension and shootings of unarmed Black men. In November of that year a "concerned citizen" called the Cleveland, Ohio, police to report seeing a person with a gun. The 9-1-1 operator was told that the person was probably a juvenile and the gun was probably a fake. This information was reportedly never passed on to the dispatcher. The police officers arrived, and one of them shot and killed Tamir Rice, a twelve-year-old Black boy who had been playing with a toy gun in the park. The police report stated that "the officers had no idea that the gun was fake or that Tamir was only 12."[1] Studies have shown that "Black boys as young as 10 may not be viewed in the same light of childhood innocence as their White peers, but are instead more likely to be mistaken as older, be perceived as guilty and face police violence if accused of a crime."[2]

As I sat in our living room in Johannesburg watching the news report, like many people of color, I experienced vicarious racial trauma and felt grief and anger over the constant racist assaults and microaggressions. I wept for Tamir's family and anxiously wondered how my own son was doing. The news story triggered a memory of when Jonathan was a child. His best friends were the Grecos, two White boys who lived across the street and were homeschooled by their mother, Dorothy. One particular day she taught on the American Revolution and staged a reenactment in which her boys dressed in uniforms and carried toy replica rifles. Her boys eagerly awaited Jonathan's return from school so they could play soldiers at the top of our dead-end street. Dorothy asked if Jonathan could join the reenactment; she even had a toy rifle for him. Without an explanation, I told her, "No, he can't play with a gun." My curt response was surprising to Dorothy, and it was educational as I explained an incident that happened to my younger brother. Years before, I had learned that play can be dangerous for Black and Brown boys, and innocent acts can quickly go sideways.

One afternoon while sitting on the front porch of our cousin's house, my brother, Ernest, was handed an unloaded BB gun. He'd held it in his hands for about five minutes when the police happened to drive by. Despite a tearful apology and explanation that the gun was not loaded, Ernest was handcuffed and shoved into the back seat of the patrol car. It was too late to post bail, so we waited until the next day to get him out of jail. When we arrived, we were told that he was now in a lineup as a suspected purse snatcher. I watched as other suspects were called in for the lineup, and several of them had distinguishing features similar to my brother. There was no way that my brother was involved in the crime. I wondered how often a Black or Brown person is in the wrong place at the wrong time, and because of a case of mistaken identity or racial bias, a life is ruined. I wept for the lost innocence of kids of color—they are seen as problems to be fixed. They aren't allowed to play with toy guns in parks or in front of houses. Their childhoods are truncated because a "concerned citizen" doesn't see them for who they are: just kids.

RACIAL BATTLE FATIGUE

I experienced vicarious trauma as I watched the nightly news reports of a racist incident, and soon I was experiencing *racial battle fatigue*, a term coined by Professor William Smith of the University of Utah. His study showed how the mental and physical stress people of color face from racism is similar to what soldiers experience in battle. He says that the stress of navigating in White spaces is "mentally, emotionally and physically draining" for people of color.[3] Every day, people of color are faced with interpreting the subtleties of microaggressions, deciphering the layers of discrimination included in the insults, and deciding whether or not to respond. The Mayo Clinic defines fatigue as "a nearly constant state of weariness that develops over time and reduces your energy, motivation and concentration."[4] People of color are frustrated and tired of fighting racism and systemic oppression. Fatigue may be the way our body alerts us to the fact that we are depressed and in need of rest.

We can relate to the children of Israel. When they were delivered out of Egypt, instead of a short journey to the Promised Land, they wandered in the desert for forty years. People of color have been given promises of equal rights and protection by the federal government that haven't been fully honored; sometimes it feels like we're also wandering in a desert without water.

Having fled from Egypt, the children of Israel were thirsty for water, and they complained to Moses: "Why did you bring us out of Egypt, to kill us and our children and livestock with thirst?" (Exodus 17:3). People of color are experiencing racial battle fatigue from the ongoing struggle against racism, and it is affecting us spiritually, emotionally, and physically. We cry out for justice in the midst of the battle, and in our spiritual fatigue we also question whether the Lord is "among us or not" (v. 7). When we are emotionally fatigued, we may feel depressed, defeated, detached, and cynical. We isolate from others and use food, drugs, or alcohol to medicate or hide our racial battle fatigue. When we are physically fatigued, our bodies bear the signs of trauma, our immune systems are weak, our appetite and sleep patterns are poor, and our bodies ache.

A recent study examined how fatigue and burnout affect racial justice activists. It found burnout to be prevalent in activists who felt responsible for eliminating structural racism. The burnout comes after the fight to overthrow structural, systemic racism and White supremacy becomes overwhelming and seemingly impossible. Some activists burn out after experiencing backlash for their activism that puts their employment or bodies at risk. Other activists of color attribute their burnout to being overwhelmed by everyday experiences of racism and microaggression.[5]

Whether an activist or not, it is exhausting and infuriating to experience racial trauma and racial battle fatigue, and there is no one to validate it. Our oppressors gaslight us by saying the racism, systemic oppression, White supremacy, and racial trauma are not real. When this happens people of color may react in several ways: flee, fold, fight, forfeit, or focus.

Flee. When we are emotionally fatigued by racism we sometimes flee. We deny, minimize, ignore, or laugh off the racism as if it doesn't matter.

When I was five, my family moved from Roxbury to a racially mixed neighborhood in Dorchester, Massachusetts. Our new house, a large Victorian, had enough room to accommodate my parents, eight siblings, and me. During the first year, one by one our White neighbors fled. Left behind were Mr. Joe and his sister, both Holocaust survivors, and our neighbors on the right, the Millers, a biracial family. Soon they all moved away as our neighborhood rapidly deteriorated.

The local trash pickups were often delayed, and the grammar school, only a couple blocks from our house, was overcrowded and underresourced. The school didn't have enough chairs and desks for its pupils. Several kids sat on the floor, hoping that somebody would be absent from school the next day so they would have a seat and a desk. Our teachers seemed disinterested, and our textbooks were old and tattered.

Fold. When people of color have to engage in a constant battle to obtain and assert our rights, we may fold in response. When we fold, we harbor self-doubt and question whether we belong, are accepted, or are acceptable. We blame ourselves because we feel we could have somehow prevented the racist act or bias. So, we create an emotional fortress to protect ourselves from further harm. As we hide in our fortress, we remain stuck with our racial trauma intact. The type of institutionalized racism endured by the Black community was a demoralizing form of emotional abuse that marginalized and racially traumatized us. Yet the Boston Public School Committee refused to acknowledge the pain and inequality faced by the Black families. The Black families of Boston's inner-city communities of Roxbury, Dorchester, and Mattapan were insignificant to the city of Boston and the school committee. The Black parents who could afford to leave the Boston school system did so by moving or enrolling their kids in a parochial school. Some parents had racial battle fatigue and just folded, figuring it was their lot in life to accept this inequitable offering. Other Black parents persevered, hoping their plight would finally be acknowledged. Then one day the Black parents had enough and rebelled.

Fight. The leaders of a parents' group persuaded and encouraged those who had racial battle fatigue to rise and fight again. In 1964 the Black parents of Boston stood firm and instituted a school boycott after repeated petitions for equal education and resources were denied by the school committee. The school committee didn't budge, and the next year, after the assassination of Malcolm X, the community once again grew weary from the battle for justice. The inspiration needed to continue the fight came on April 22, 1965, when Dr. Martin Luther King Jr. led a civil rights march in Boston. He started the rally by proclaiming, "This is not a battle of White people against Black people." He said, "It is a struggle between the forces of justice and injustice."[6] As the rain fell, the group marched toward Boston Common loudly singing freedom songs like "We Shall Overcome." That day about twenty-two thousand folks gathered to hear MLK speak about de facto racism and racial segregation in education and housing in Massachusetts. The march was a galvanizing point that emboldened the Black community to engage in more targeted activism. The community determined to no longer be ignored; they committed to continue the fight to obtain a quality education for their kids.

However, the school committee chairwoman, Louise Day Hicks, insisted that the schools in the Black community were more than adequate. Her attempt to gaslight the Black community failed in the summer of 1965 after community activists called for a parent meeting at the Robert Gould Shaw House in Roxbury. My parents attended the meeting. They sat on cold metal chairs on the edge of the room near the door and listened intently. The room was full, with about 250 parents complaining about the education or the lack thereof their children received. The parents soon discovered an open enrollment policy that allowed any child to attend a school outside their neighborhood if there was an open seat. The parents agreed there should be a mass exodus of Black students to fill the seven thousand open seats throughout the city.

Martin Luther King Jr. often cited the story of the Israelites' enslavement and exodus from Egypt. He said, "Whenever men [and women] have thought seriously of life, they have dreamed of a promised land."[7] He spoke of the Promised Land as a metaphor for the freedom journey of Black folks in this country. It also mirrors the hardships that many other people of color have endured. In the story Pharaoh is the living embodiment of systemic racism set up to resist God's plan for people of color. Initially, Pharaoh hardened his heart against the Lord's specific demand that the Israelites be allowed to leave Egypt with their families and all of their goods and possessions. Pharaoh's message to the Israelites: "Okay, you can go, but not very far." "Okay, but only the men, not the women and kids." "Okay, you can take your families too, but not your possessions." Like Moses, we have confronted Pharaoh and oppressive systems with God's command: "Let my people go," but Pharaoh has refused. The Black parents believed the fight for the education of their kids was a fight for freedom from bondage under the rule of the Boston Public School Committee. Operation Exodus was born as the Black community stood up, and in one voice proclaimed to the school committee, "Let our children go."

The journey out of Egypt was not an easy one. In the wilderness Moses cried out to the Lord to provide water for the thirsty children of Israel. God responds to Moses, "'Take in your hand the staff with which you struck the Nile, and go. I will stand there before you by the rock at Horeb. Strike the rock, and water will come out of it for the people to drink.' So, Moses did this in the sight of the elders of Israel" (Exodus 17:5-6 NIV).

The Boston Public School Committee seemed like an unmovable rock until the Operation Exodus parents struck it and justice began to flow. These committed parents thought outside the box, and with prayer and fortitude, they obtained what was rightfully theirs. After many delays, just weeks before the start of school, the school committee released a list of thousands of open seats in schools across the city. The school department put up roadblocks, giving misinformation about the location of the vacant seats and unlawfully mandating personal interviews before admission. Despite the obstacles, the Black parents rushed to enroll their kids in the neighboring White schools.

My parents enrolled me, my sister Stephanie, and brother Kwame in an all-White school in North Dorchester. The night before the first day of school Momae used the hot comb on our hair lathered with Sulphur 8 Hair Pomade to straighten our tight coils. She parted our hair in two sections then gathered them into two ponytails. Our best dresses were ironed and laid out for school. In the morning we stood in front of the gray house on the corner of Bernard and Harvard Streets waiting for a yellow school bus to arrive and transport us to the promised land. The bus monitor, Mrs. Green, told us to get in line: "No shoving. Wait for your turn." Kwame took a seat in the back of the bus, and I sat next to Stephanie with my wide eyes fixed forward. The bus pulled up in front of the school, and from the window I saw White mothers dropping off their kids. Some glared at us, and others shook their heads seemingly in disgust. There were no protest signs or cursing, possibly because the infiltration of only a handful of Black kids was tolerable. At the top of the granite stairs stood Dr. Hurley, a somewhat round White woman wearing a powdery blue dress, black kitten heels, her hair in a beehive, and bejeweled cat-eye glasses precariously perched on her nose. Dr. Hurley wore reddish lipstick but no smile. She feigned a greeting, and we were ushered to our classrooms. My teacher introduced me to my first-grade classmates, but all I can remember was twenty-five White faces with their eyes fixed on me.

During that first week Kwame's teacher repeatedly called him Tyrone. His classmates mocked him during his outside recess period. They poked out their bottom lip so it covered their top lip and chanted, "Look, nigger lips." During my recess my classmates invited me to join them in a game where one of them was blindfolded and felt my face and hair to guess who I was. There were only two students with broad noses and hair slick with pomade now returning to its tightly coiled state. It was easy to guess it was either Stephanie or me. This childhood game may have been innocent enough, but for me, it highlighted my otherness and at the same time showed me how Black girls are interchangeable.

My parents hoped that the playing field would be level and we would realize that we were as strong academically as Becky or Billy. But the White educators seemed bent on reminding us that this couldn't possibly be true.

Fold. I remember three incidents when both Stephanie and I folded. One day Stephanie made the mistake of telling her teacher that her tow-haired classmate Bobby had just called her nigger. Bobby was not punished; instead the teacher dragged Stephanie to the porcelain sink in the classroom and washed her mouth out with soap powder for repeating the word. It seemed our teachers wanted to extinguish any vestige of self-esteem in us.

A few weeks later there was a substitute teacher in Stephanie's class, and at the start of her lesson she asked the students what they wanted to be when they grew up. Stephanie raised her hand and patiently waited to be recognized. When she was finally called on, she stood proudly and proclaimed, "When I grow up I want to be a teacher." The teacher snorted, "That won't happen. They won't hire a nigger as a teacher." Stephanie slumped down in her chair; she, along with her hopes and dreams, was irrelevant to the teacher. Stephanie wasn't the only one who felt this way.

I was a timid, quiet child who consistently performed well on tests, but I also was unseen. My teachers often accused me of cheating. In their minds cheating was the only way I could possibly get such high marks. The suspicion was not limited to academics. The day after Stephanie's classroom humiliation, I sat in my chair busily doing my schoolwork when my classmate Timmy walked by and tripped over his own feet. However, he cried out, "Sheila tripped me!" The teacher immediately seized on this accusation and demanded that I apologize for intentionally causing him to fall. I was stunned and repeatedly declared my innocence. She hammered her response to "apologize to him. Do it now." Then she raised the stakes and demanded: "Sheila, get up here in front of the class and apologize to Timmy!" Through heaving sobs, I apologized for something I didn't do.

In school, I tried to fit in and feel at home in my own body. I wanted to believe that I was more than just my skin color and that I deserved to be treated as an equal. But that day I folded. I learned it was better to go along to get along, to stay quiet and accept that I was ignored by White people. My mind complied, but my body didn't bear the stress well. I started having physical symptoms: hives, frequent ear infections, and headaches. Some days I received a reprieve and was kept at home from school. I made my false peace treaty and just stuffed my pain, anger, and fear about the riot and my schooling, only to have the racial trauma later resurface. By the end of that school year, after allegations that Stephanie had repeatedly cheated on her tests, my parents were informed that she wasn't promoted and would have to repeat the third grade. Nevertheless, I held onto a shred of hope that one day I'd be accepted or at least not be bullied and shamed.

The Operation Exodus program continued, yet it began to see a decline in donor funding. By the time I reached middle school, Operation Exodus could no longer afford to rent buses, so we had to find our own way to school. Some parents carpooled, and older kids like me took public transportation. The Washington Irving Middle School, to my delight, had three staff of color and teachers who seemed to want to be there. I had an excellent English teacher. Mrs. Shakespeare wore long, flowing dresses like a flower child from the 1960s. She said we could all be poets and writers. I believed her. Then one day as I listened to her rave over a short story written by my White classmate Siobhan, I began to question the quality of my writing. Again, I folded, and for a season shut down my desire to write. By the end of the school year, as I looked forward to attending Roslindale High School, Operation Exodus also folded.

Fight. After receiving the miraculous provision of water, we read in Exodus that the Israelites faced a new fight. The Amalekites came and attacked them at Rephidim. Moses told Joshua, "Choose some of our men and go out to fight the Amalekites. Tomorrow I will stand on top of the hill with the staff of God in my hands." Moses, Aaron, and Hur stood at the top of the hill. "As long as Moses held up his hands, the Israelites were winning, but whenever he lowered his hands, the Amalekites were winning" (Exodus 17:9, 11 NIV). Like Moses, our hands and hearts grow weary in this protracted fight for reconciliation and social justice. This is not the time to give up or give in, but we desperately need renewed strength from God so we do not lose the battle.

As I transitioned to high school, things were also shifting in the city—a new fight was unfolding. On June 21, 1974, Judge Arthur Garrity ruled that the school officials intentionally maintained de facto segregation in the Boston schools, which was against the law. The ruling mandated that school administrators and teachers be reassigned to different schools based on their race. The city now had to bus some eighteen thousand Black, White, and Brown kids into neighboring communities to desegregate those schools.

The summer before busing was to take full effect my mother sent Stephanie to live with our grandparents in Virginia to avoid her assignment at a poorly performing school in Roxbury. Prior to the start of the school year we moved to Dorchester Lower Mills, and over the summer we were informed that my brother Salahaldin was assigned to Hyde Park High School. By September the busing era in Boston began and ushered in a protracted season of protests and violence primarily in the communities of South Boston, Charlestown, Hyde Park, and to a lesser degree in Roxbury. In October the *Boston Globe* newspaper reported, "What we prayed wouldn't happen has happened. The city of Boston has gotten out of control."[8]

Each day during the first few months at Roslindale High, we endured the harassment of a small group of anti-busing protesters across the street from the school. However, at Hyde Park High over the course of two years, Salahaldin and the other Black kids offloaded and boarded their school buses while dodging rocks and swear words hurled by White parents and kids. Almost every day racially motivated fights erupted inside the school building, often because of a minor slight such as one person's backpack brushing up against somebody. Salahaldin's girlfriend, Lauren, could not reconcile how she and classmate Susie worked well as partners in science class, but after school Susie stood next to her mom with a brick in her hand.

In 1976 Roslindale High closed down, and my brother Kwame, sister Makeda, and I were assigned to a newly built high school in West Roxbury. Although our experience at West Roxbury High was relatively peaceful, I carried racial trauma from my past and vicarious trauma from Salahaldin's experience. I often wondered if our new school would eventually devolve into chaos.

Most of our teachers seemed to care about the current and future success of all the students, including the Black ones. Our school had Black educators such as Rodger Harris, a Vietnam vet who was featured in Ken Burns's film on the Vietnam War. They helped us navigate the vicarious trauma we experienced from listening to friends and family recounting what was happening at their other schools. The one exception was a White guidance counselor who told me, "Don't bother applying to Tufts because you won't get in." I was determined to prove him wrong. I studied hard for my SAT exam and later was accepted into Tufts University with a full scholarship. We felt safe inside our school, but outside there were communities across the city that we dared not visit.

Forfeit. A year later I graduated in the first senior class under busing in Boston. A national news outlet ran a story that compared the relative calm at my high school with other schools in the city. The only difference I saw between the schools is that at my high school, some of the Black students had been a part of Operation Exodus. The Black and White students had known one another since middle school; we played on the same sports teams and developed friendships, so there was less fear of one another. I graduated high school hopeful and excited about my future. I would be the first of my siblings to attend college.

Racial battle fatigue can lead to forfeiting who we are and what we want and need. We will even make a false peace treaty and perform and submit to meet other people's expectations. I learned early on to trust no one with my interior life, so it was years before I could see and share what happened and continued to happen to my people and me. In autumn 1977, Mom and Aunt Sereta Ann drove me to Tufts University. It was about an hour from home but felt like another world. I was in culture shock living among so many White, Black, and Brown students from upper-middle class and wealthy families. I wanted to fit in badly, so I hid the fact that I came from a poor working family, had no financial support, and had to work part time. Like other students of color, I felt I had to code-switch when interacting with Whites on campus. I changed how and what I spoke about so I was more acceptable to the dominant White culture.

My story is not unlike other first-generation students of color who enter majority White institutions: I didn't know how to ask for help. I thought that I should know how to succeed in college, and because I didn't, I carried a lot of shame. Many of us believe there is a stigma associated with our first-generation status, and we fear we will be seen as having a deficit. So we choose to suffer in silence rather than to ask for help.[9] *Stereotype threat* is a term coined by social scientists Claude Steele and Joshua Aronson.[10] Stereotype threat occurs when people of color unconsciously fear living up to a negative stereotype about their group. Instead of trying to prevent this, people self-sabotage, disengage, or alter their aspirations, which ironically causes them to live up to the feared stereotype.

During my first year in college, I experienced stereotype threat. I self-sabotaged by missing classes and submitting late assignments. I almost flunked out and fulfilled the stereotype that Black, Latina, and Latino students are not college material. I wondered if my high school guidance counselor was right in questioning my application to Tufts. My first-semester grade report was a wake-up call. I had to look at how my thinking needed to change, and I started to fight to stay enrolled at Tufts. I attended the tutorials and got support from my peers. After four years I was shy one course to graduate, but I was exhausted and procrastinating.

I was responding like other first-generation students of color: I was experiencing "break away" guilt, a phenomenon that happens when the decision to attend and graduate from college comes with a relational cost.[11] On some level I felt I was abandoning my family and community. I had to face the fact that I was standing in my own way. But I had to decide if I was going to fold, flee, fight, or continue to forfeit. I chose the good fight for my future and accepted help to push through my fears to complete the course and graduate. Five years after graduation I obtained a master's degree in counseling, and four years later I married Nick and then had two kids, Jonathan and Alexia. Yet it took some time before I realized I still carried the racial trauma and internalized shame into adulthood.

Focus. My journey of healing has not been a straight line. Sometimes I've lost my focus on God. It was three steps forward and one step back before the healing set in. In my weariness I've cried out in words written in the book of Jeremiah:

Is there no balm in Gilead?
Is there no physician there?
Why then is there no healing
for the wound of my people? (Jeremiah 8:22 NIV)

And I found healing in unexpected ways.

While Moses stood upholding the staff in his hand, he was not alone. Aaron and Hur were with him, and they witnessed his struggle with fatigue. When Moses' hands grew tired, they provided the support he needed. They found a rock and put it underneath Moses so he could sit. Then they held up his hands—one on each side—so his hands remained steady till sunset. Because of his faithful companions, Israel won the battle.

In the past when I experienced racial battle fatigue, the Lord brought healing refreshment to me through people. Sometimes I was surprised when simple acts of acceptance or resistance brought healing. Early in my marriage, God provided faithful companions at Bethel AME (African Methodist Episcopal) Church. There I was reminded in Word and song that "there is a balm in Gilead to make the wounded whole": Jesus. In that community there was space to sit and rest, encounter Jesus, refuel, and go back to continue to fight. Like many predominantly Black churches, Bethel is a place where I could be unapologetically myself, a Black woman who didn't have to explain herself, justify her existence, or code-switch. It was the first church our kids attended where there were Black folk from all walks of life. Our kids saw Jesus minister his healing balm through the community, passionate Gospel songs, dancing in the Holy Spirit, prayer, and call-and-response during sermons. They saw in Christ and community that all things are possible.

Our parenting journey in that season was healing for me. Our church family helped us to persevere and be empowered by the Lord. Nick and I were able to reject the labels that the world put on our kids and us. When I was young, I couldn't tell my parents what I endured at school, and if I had I wasn't sure they'd do anything about it. I had to release to God the unforgiveness I held toward my parents for what I believed they should have known and done for me. I gained a greater sense of freedom, no longer feeling racial battle fatigue, sad, and powerless. This contributed to our kids being able to open up to us about the racism they were experiencing at school. I had a renewed strength to pray, persevere, and act on our kids' behalf.

A few years later I had another experience of healing from racial battle fatigue that involved dealing with my unforgiveness. While attending an emotional healing conference, the main speaker concluded his remarks by asking all the people of color to come forward. I and seven Black, biracial, Latinx, and Asian believers stood in a row in front of the stage. The speaker talked about our fatigue as we've struggled to reach our own people and for acceptance in the majority culture. He apologized on behalf of White folks and encouraged us to take our rightful place in God's kingdom. As he spoke and prayed, he wept along with several of us. However, I remained stoic until we took Communion.

As I held the bread and wine in my hand and focused on what Jesus had done, tears began to flow, and soon my blouse was wet. I was taken aback by my response. Yes, there have been White folks who've said they were sorry about slavery and present-day racism. But this was different. Hebrews 12:3 says, "Consider him who endured such hostility against himself from sinners, so that you may not grow weary or lose heart." I realized after the conference that this was the first time I felt that my experience, weariness, and pain were seen and validated by a White person. I later shared this with the speaker, and we both wept again. Before the conference I would've said that I dealt with the wounds inflicted by my racist teachers and that I handled current incidents of racism and micro-aggressions quite well. In reality I had dealt with this only in part. I wanted an apology that I would never get. In time, however, God brought it up again, as if to ask, "Now, will you deal with all of it? Will you?" That day I finally did it.

Racism is relentless. It's likely in the future that we will experience racial battle fatigue or weariness from yet another racial conversation or be deeply grieved by a racial incident. If and when this happens and we are weary, we need to remember that we do not have sufficient power to rescue or to save anyone, including ourselves. Jesus tells us, "Come to me, all you that are weary and are carrying heavy burdens, and I will give you rest. Take my yoke upon you, and learn from me; for I am gentle and humble in heart, and you will find rest for your souls. For my yoke is easy, and my burden is light" (Matthew 11:28-30). We can combat racial battle fatigue and also lighten our loads by taking care of our health, or we become vulnerable to racial battle fatigue simply because we fail to do the basics: eating well, getting sleep, and exercising. If we know that specific situations trigger racial battle fatigue, we can try to avoid those stressful setups. Sometimes we can't prevent them, but we can limit our intake of social media and despairing conversations, and rather save our energy for the battles that lie ahead. Taking time to experience the beauty around us in art and nature and prioritizing life-affirming relationships can help accelerate healing and recovery. We need others who will help us to identify any negative patterns in our lives and encourage us to take proactive steps to avoid and manage fatigue. When we face racially charged situations with our focus on the Lord, we see that we are not alone or powerless; we can choose to stay or flee, get real or forfeit, stand or fold, surrender or fight.

REFLECTION AND PRAYER PROMPTS

1. How has racial battle fatigue affected your life?

2. What heavy burden are you now carrying? Pray and release it to the Lord. Exchange your burden for the Lord's.

3. What kind of support do you need right now?

CHAPTER THREE

SILENCE

While I kept silence,
my body wasted away
through my groaning all day long.

PSALM 32:3

In the wake of Japan's attack on Pearl Harbor, signs began appearing on restaurants and shop windows: "No Japs Served Here!" Two months later President Franklin D. Roosevelt signed Executive Order 9066, which resulted in the relocation of United States citizens of Japanese ancestry into internment camps. Little attention was paid to the impact that internment would have on Japanese American individuals, families, and communities. Nori's grandparents and their three kids had less than two weeks before they were forced out of their Los Angeles home. His grandparents owned an apartment complex, and with such short notice they had no choice but to sell the property at a cut rate to unscrupulous Caucasian buyers. Most Japanese families were in shock as they left their homes with only the clothes on their back or as much as they could carry.[1] The kids were traumatized by the unbearable loss of their friends and classmates. There would be no home waiting for them if they were ever to return.

Contrary to US military propaganda films, most Japanese families did not see internment as their civic or heroic duty. The narrative that they gladly surrendered their homes, community, and livelihood for the sake of their safety and for our country was false. Christians were mostly silent about the injustice. It seemed their love for their Japanese neighbors waned while their fear of them grew. Floyd Schmoe, a White Quaker antiwar activist, was one exception. He forcefully spoke up for the Japanese community, stating that "justice cannot be done by branding all men, who by the accident of their birth, come from countries now at war with the United States, as enemy aliens."[2] There were few public protests against internment, and in some instances they were rooted in racism. Governor Chase Clark of Idaho stated, "Japs live like rats, breathe like rats, and act like rats," and insisted that the Japanese not be interned in Idaho. Historian William Manchester writes of how many other public figures openly referred to Japanese Americans in offensive and stereotypical terms. The Nevada Bar Association resolved, "We feel that if Japs are dangerous in Berkeley, California, they are likewise dangerous in the state of Nevada," and Governor Homer M. Adkins from Arkansas followed by announcing, "Our people are not familiar with the customs or peculiarities of the Japanese, and I doubt the wisdom of placing any in Arkansas."[3]

Despite the racist opposition to the proposed locations of the camps, our government opened ten internment camps between 1942 and 1945. About 120,000 Japanese Americans were held in California, Arizona, Wyoming, Colorado, Utah, and Arkansas. Nori's dad was six years old when he and his extended family members arrived at the Heart Mountain Relocation Center in Fort Hood, Wyoming. The center was surrounded by a high fence topped with barbed wire, and a sentry tower was strategically positioned with armed guards ready to shoot to kill anyone attempting to escape. The message was clear: This wasn't a relocation center; it was a prison camp. The internees were to remain quiet, obedient, and in fear of the guards who dealt swiftly with any infraction. The guards at the internment camps were given license to act forcefully to quell any disobedience, escape attempts, or plots of treason. A few guards were tried for excessive force. One guard was tried for killing sixty-three-year-old chef James Hatsuki Wakasa. The guard claimed that Mr. Wakasa had tried to escape. However, Mr. Wakasa was not running away from the guard but walking toward him when shot. The guard was found not guilty. Another guard was tried for killing Shoichi James Okamoto. The guard was acquitted and fined one dollar for unauthorized use of government property, the cost of the bullet he used to kill Mr. Okamoto.[4] For over three years Nori's family endured life in the cold and desolate camp. The lack of privacy, communal toilets and showers, and overcrowding strained most relationships. The internees tried to bring normalcy to their lives through activities such as sewing and music concerts, and some held menial jobs in the camp. Dr. Satsuki Ina reports that "the Japanese cultural values of *gaman* (endure), *gambaru* (persevere), *giri* (duty), *oyakoko* (filial piety), and *kodomo no tame ni* (sacrifice) guided and helped family members to endure the shame, hardship, and tragedy of being incarcerated and deemed risks to the national security."[5]

Meanwhile, a few churches ministered in the camps, and some Japanese internees converted to Christianity. However, Nori's dad was not one of them. He found no savior to rescue him from the years of brutality he endured at the hands of the older boys in the camp. By the end of 1945, all of the camps were ordered closed. For some internees those Japanese cultural values had morphed into the psychological defense mechanisms of repressing, denying, and rationalizing the significance of the racial trauma. This was the case for Nori's dad.

COPING

The racism experienced by the Japanese continued after their release. A sign appeared on the house in a majority White neighborhood: "Japs Keep Moving, This Is a White Neighborhood." Nori's family moved back to Los Angeles but found they could not afford to live in their former community. The family ended up in Skid Row, an impoverished and dangerous neighborhood plagued by alcohol and violence. In the midst of the pervasive fear and instability in the community, Nori's grandfather worked hard to reclaim what they lost. He worked tirelessly managing and repairing several old crumbling properties without any help. His stress mounted as he had to also deal with difficult and dangerous tenants while trying to meet the needs of his family. The internment and the adverse effects of racial trauma also had an impact on his physical health.

Gwendolyn M. Jensen conducted a survey of former internees and found that in addition to psychological struggles, internees had over twice the risk of cardiovascular disease, mortality, and premature death than those who were not interned.[6] In addition to the formerly interned Japanese Americans and their kids, other people of color have also experienced systemic and institutional racism, and the racial trauma affects on our bodies. Dr. Staggers-Hakim reports, "When people are constantly worried about experiencing racism or are consistently exposed to racism directly, at work, for example, or through witnessing state-sanctioned violence such as police brutality, over time, the stress causes wear and tear on the body making people vulnerable to a host of acute (cold or flu) and chronic diseases."[7]

The Center for Disease Control reports that the risk of pregnancy-related deaths for Black women is three to four times higher than those of White women. This disparity is due to the extreme stress that Black women have carried over generations and the systemic racism that affects the quality of medical care received. The day after tennis great Serena Williams gave birth via cesarean section, she had trouble breathing and "alerted a nurse to what she felt was happening in her body and asked for a CT scan and a blood thinner, but the nurse suggested that pain medication had perhaps left Ms. Williams confused." Serena insisted, "but a doctor instead performed an ultrasound of her legs." She had a history of a pulmonary embolism, and after demanding a CT scan, it was discovered that indeed she had a pulmonary embolism. If Serena had not persisted, she would likely have died.[8]

Bessel A. van der Kolk wrote, "It takes tremendous energy to keep functioning while carrying the memory of terror, and the shame of utter weakness and vulnerability."[9]

This is as true for us as it was for the woman with the issue of blood recorded in Mark 5:24-34. A large crowd followed and pressed around Jesus. A woman was there who had been suffering from hemorrhages for twelve years. She came up behind Jesus in the crowd and touched his cloak, because she thought, "If I just touch his clothes, I will be healed" (v. 28 NIV). If we apply the law written in Leviticus 15, the woman would be considered unclean, so Jesus' interaction with her would make him ceremonially unclean until the evening.

Asian Americans and other people of color have endured years of racism that have deemed us unwanted and unclean. We've experienced spiritual, emotional, and physical hemorrhaging from racial trauma. Because we emotionally battle with shame and fear, we hide our vulnerability. We silently hope for healing or create our own coping mechanisms. The research of Dr. Sherman James into health disparities among African Americans identified a coping mechanism used to combat ongoing psychosocial and environmental stress, stigma, and racism. Dr. James reported that when people are "'really trying to make ends meet going up against very powerful forces of dislocation—their biological systems are going to pay a price,' he said. 'That's the situation African Americans have been in since the beginning,' he added. 'Now we're seeing other groups begin to be exposed to these same forces.'"[10] Dr. James named the John Henryism Hypotheses after his patient John Henry Martin, who rose from being a sharecropper to become a wealthy farmer with seventy-five acres of land. Like the mythical John Henry of folklore who died of exhaustion after beating a mechanical steam drill, Dr. James's patient also paid a hefty price for overworking. His patient was afflicted with hypertension, arthritis, and a severe peptic ulcer, and his physical health continued to decline. Dr. James developed the John Henry scale to identify those who have physically suffered as a result of their constant striving.

Although not an African American, Nori's grandfather would likely have rated high on the John Henryism scale. By the age of fifty-eight, Nori's grandfather died of a heart attack while making repairs in the apartment building. His family attributed his death to heartbreak, overwork, stress, and the internment.

SILENT

Elie Wiesel says, "We must always take sides. Neutrality helps the oppressor, never the victim. Silence encourages the tormentor, never the tormented."[11]

Nori's dad never spoke of how he coped with the death of his father. However, his family saw a further shutting down emotionally. Although he felt a deep connection to the Japanese American community, the harsh experience of internment made it difficult for him to trust people. Nori's dad could not share the extent of the abuse he suffered. He would only sit as others talked about their experiences in the camps. Nobu Miyoshi writes, "One of the most hauntingly pressing issues facing Japanese Americans today is their concentration camp experience during World War II."

Yet, the major groups of survivors—the Nisei—generally do not confront the implications of it within themselves or with their own children. . . . [T]hey remain confused or even injured by the traumatic experience."[12] A few years after Nori's mom immigrated to the United States, she met and married his dad, who brought his silence with him into the marriage. Within a few years Nori was born, followed by his sister, Katsu. When Nori was seven years old, he realized that his dad was "hemorrhaging" not only emotionally but also physically. His dad's silent screams left marks on his body.

Van der Kolk notes, "As long as you keep secrets and suppress information, you are fundamentally at war with yourself. . . . The critical issue is allowing yourself to know what you know. That takes an enormous amount of courage."[13] Nori's dad was afflicted with unbearable hives, which covered his entire back. Like many survivors of racial trauma, his way of handling his pain and fear was to try to medicate or numb it. Nori's dad chose to medicate himself with alcohol. Over time his drinking increased as did the fights, yelling, and instances of domestic violence. Katsu was fearful of her dad; she and her mom would bar the door with a two-by-four at night to stop him from coming into the house drunk. After one argument when Nori's dad put his hands around their mom's neck, Katsu kept a kitchen knife hidden in her bedside dresser for self-protection.

When Nori came to Christ during his junior year of high school, his dad raised questions about God and the internment. He asked, "Nori, where was Christ when we were incarcerated?" "Why were White Christians applauding that?" Nori had no response. He merely wondered, *What would Dad have been like if the internment never happened or if he was able to give voice to his pain?* For much of his life, Nori carried the heavy weight of his family dysfunction. He feared that at any moment his dad would once again verbally or physically abuse his mom or Katsu. He felt overly responsible not only for them but also in other ways. There was an unspoken expectation that he would be a model minority and bring honor to his family.

MODEL MINORITY

The stereotype of Asian Americans as model minorities emerged after the US immigration laws changed to officially allow them to immigrate into the United States. Many of these new arrivals were highly educated and skilled. The model minorities were supposedly quiet, compliant, studious, aspirational, wealthy, and wise. The US fixation on money as the chief measure of success negates other vital achievements such as physical, spiritual, relational, and emotional health. Although some Asians have a healthy financial status, many carry heavy emotional and relational burdens to become a model minority. Sociologist Rosalind Chou found that "when Asian Americans are depicted as the minority group that doesn't complain, attract negative attention, or cause problems, it can feel uncomfortable for them to point out stereotypes, insults, and assaults."[14]

The model-minority stereotype persists to this day, and it silences the voices of our Asian American sisters and brothers. At times it also pits them against African Americans and other people of color. The *Washington Post* reported that "the greatest thing that ever happened to Asian Americans wasn't that they studied hard, or that they benefited from tiger moms or Confucian values. It's that other Americans started treating them with a little more respect."[15] Chhaya Chhoum, executive director of Mekong NYC, asserts that "research often treats Asian-Americans as monolithic and ignores the diversity of their experiences in the United States." Many Southeast Asian Americans are "invisibles and [are] living in many intersections of oppression."[16] The respect accorded other Asians in the United States is often not given to Southeast Asian

Americans who have not obtained the same level of success because they may live in poorer communities, face language barriers, and lack access to quality education. It's important to note that the respect other Asian Americans receive doesn't always translate into success and job promotion. The *Atlantic* reported that Asian Americans with high paying jobs "still encounter discrimination that can block their path to the highest professional tiers."[17] Nori's dad experienced this type of racial bias at the job he held for almost thirty years. He watched his White colleagues rise in the ranks while he hit the proverbial glass ceiling. He was never promoted to any senior-level position within the company. The bias at work increased Nori's dad's stress levels, led to even more drinking, and made his marriage all the more volatile. While Nori was in college, his parents separated and then divorced.

GENERATIONAL TRAUMA

The trauma experienced by the survivors of internment may directly or indirectly affect their children. Donna K. Nagata writes,

> Despite the silence, or perhaps because of it, the Sansei who had a parent interned felt the effects of that experience in numerous ways. They are sad and angry about the injustice and attribute some negative consequences in their own lives to their parents' internment. These include feelings of low self-esteem, the pressure to assimilate, an accelerated loss of the Japanese culture and language, and experiencing the unexpressed pain of their parents.[18]

Like his dad, Nori had a hard time knowing how he felt about things because he spent so much time navigating his dad's emotions and behavior. Yet he also feared that he'd become like his dad, whose treatment of women was confusing and disturbing. Nori was also afflicted in other ways.

He has an aversion to feeling buzzed, remembering his mom's words, "Don't be like your father." The need for control sometimes meant Nori found himself emulating his dad by emotionally shutting down or being silently manipulative to get what he wanted. Meanwhile, Katsu depended heavily on her mom, who protected her but also criticized her constantly for perceived imperfections like walking slowly or daydreaming. Katsu became a hard worker in her own way, but her relationship with her mom became strained, in part because of the way their relationship had been so influenced by her dad's anger, emotional absence, and alcoholism. Both Katsu and Nori now realize as adults that they do a great job brushing their teeth because it was the only thing their mom praised their dad for.

THE LOS ANGELES RIOTS

In 1988 Congress issued a formal apology for the internment. Over one hundred thousand Japanese Americans received $20,000 each as reparations for their material loss and suffering. Nori's dad and grandmother received payments, which helped the family financially. It was an emotional and exhilarating time for Japanese Americans, and everyone was talking about it.

Along with others, Nori's family hoped that the reparation would permanently put the past to rest. Nori thought that maybe our country's racial problems were solved, but the Rodney King incident revealed otherwise.

On the night of March 3, 1991, officers of the Los Angeles Police Department pulled over Rodney King for a traffic violation. He reportedly resisted an arrest, which prompted four arresting officers to beat him savagely with their nightsticks. An amateur video emerged showing each of the fifty blows that were inflicted on King. A year later the officers were tried for the use of excessive force, and the jury came back with a not guilty verdict, which absolved the four police officers. Within hours of hearing the decision, the Black community was enraged and rioted in protest.

The businesses of many Los Angeles Korean Americans were looted and burned. Nori listened intently to the radio interviews of leaders in the White, Black, and Korean communities as they expressed sadness and anger and accusations. It became clear to him that he was ignorant about the history and lives of African Americans in this country. He remembered that his dad had once told him, "Nori, you should always feel grateful for the Black community, because the reason why we are where we're at is mostly because of them." His dad understood the significance of the civil rights movement and had admiration for Dr. Martin Luther King Jr. and Bobby Kennedy. As Nori listened to members of the Black community, he began to question why the Japanese internment was the only thing the US government has officially apologized for and paid reparation. How was the Japanese Americans' internment any different from the Black, Asian, Latinx, and First Nation communities affected by systemic racism, slavery, antimiscegenation laws, forced removals, and land-ownership laws? His questions went unanswered. Many of his White and East Asian friends at college didn't seem to care about injustice. One day, while praying and crying out to God about the systemic oppression of people of color, Nori felt Jesus say to him, "Let's do something about this, you and me."

HIS STORY

Before Nori was free to do something about what he saw, he had to deal with his past. Like the woman with the issue of blood, he needed healing. As the woman touched the hem of Jesus' garment, her bleeding immediately stopped, and she felt in her body that she was free from her suffering. When Jesus realized that power had gone out from him, he turned around in the crowd and asked,

"'Who touched my clothes?' 'You see the people crowding against you,' his disciples answered, 'and yet you can ask, "Who touched me?""" (Mark 5:30-31 NIV). Jesus kept looking around to see who had touched him. Regardless of the consequences, Jesus stopped and waited for the woman to show herself and to tell her story, her whole truth.

While in college Nori's healing began as he told his story, his whole truth about the impact of his father's internment and the wounds of racial trauma. Nori's most significant healing happened when he opened up to a few insightful and prayerful mentors. Most significant was a Japanese American Christian who was also from a divorced family. During one year, Nori met with friends each week to read and pray through a book by a Christian counselor. Sometimes he sat on the overstuffed sofa and listened, and several times he wept as he shared his family's story, uncovering and confronting his pain. After graduating college, Nori continued on his journey of healing; for over three years he researched the internment, spoke with family members, read more books about trauma, and prayed alone and with friends.

The healing path led to the way of forgiveness. Over time Nori forgave FDR for the internment order and White society in general for being complicit. The apostle John says, "The commandment we have from him is this: those who love God must love their brothers and sisters also" (1 John 4:21). For there to be a restoration of relationships in his family, Nori realized that he needed to release his dad from judgment. Nori had to forgive his dad for what he did and did not do in the past. This happened in stages. Eventually, the cords of unforgiveness were cut, and Nori was free. Just as Jesus received and blessed the woman who for over a decade was deemed an outcast and unclean, Nori was able to love, bless, and accept his dad.

Jesus freed the woman with the issue of blood from her agony and isolation. He bestowed peace and shalom to her. When Jesus publicly proclaimed the woman as a daughter healed and cleansed, he upheld her dignity and restored her to the community. Nori's emotional affliction lifted as he felt the depth of love and acceptance Christ has for him. He then became committed to loving others more deeply.

SOCIAL JUSTICE

It has been noted that "the internment sensitized Japanese Americans to issues of social justice. Today, years after the successful redress effort, multiple generations of Japanese Americans remain watchful of policies and prejudices that unjustly target other groups."[19] In James 2:14-17 we read, "What good is it, my brothers and sisters, if you say you have faith but do not have works? Can faith save you? If a brother or sister is naked and lacks daily food, and one of you says to them, 'Go in peace; keep warm and eat your fill,' and yet you do not supply their bodily needs, what is the good of that? So, faith by itself, if it has no works, is dead."

Nori put his faith into action after graduating from college. He worked at a Fortune 500 company but chose to live among Mexican immigrant families in a city that, at the time, had one of the highest per-capita murder rates in the nation.

Nori was mentored by a couple who ministered to those families. He played worship music for their weekly Bible study. Nori cared about the people and saw the image of God in them and how precious their families were to the Lord. He fostered mentor-mentee relationships where he could honestly confront the issues of race, class, and culture within and outside of himself. Many myths Nori held about the poor died as he lived and served in his community. Although the challenges to overcome personal and systemic oppression were great, he refused to give up, lose faith, or lose sight of the kingdom of God.

After working at the same company for six years, Nori moved to Boston. He married Jia, and they bought a house in the second highest crime area in Boston. The three-family house is home to them and their two kids, and the other units are rentals that are at below-market rent. For several years Asian, Black, White, and Latinx Christian friends, teachers, and social workers have lived in the house and have formed a Christian community. Their mission can be summed up in Psalm 107:41: "He raises up the needy out of distress, and makes their families like flocks." While living and serving in this inner-city community, Nori's healing continues. The Lord has increased his family; it's now an ethnically diverse, ministry-oriented one committed to blessing the neighborhood and the city. There is a community garden where neighbors gather, laugh, and share the fruit of their labor. The garden is also a source of healthy food for the community in an area known as a food desert because there are few full-service grocery stores. It is also located in a food swamp, an area with lots of high calorie fast-food establishments. One study suggests that "the presence of a food swamp is a stronger predictor of obesity rates than the absence of full-service grocery stores."[20] The simple addition of a community garden helps reduce obesity rates and the resulting afflictions.

Nori's family attends a neighborhood church of mostly Black and pan-African neighbors. They have Bible studies in which they discuss how urgent topics like mass incarceration affect them and what the Scriptures have to say about it. They talk about the need for homeownership and debt reduction to stave off the threat of gentrification, which is pushing poor people of color out of the city. They pray about what they need to say and do about what they see.

We have much to learn from Nori, Jia, their two kids, and their Christian community. We can refuse to be silenced and reclaim our voice. We can let others into our inner life. We can link arms with other people of color and commit to doing what seems like small acts of faith and love in and through Christ. Yet these acts are cumulatively having a significant impact on the lives of many folks in the community.

REFLECTION AND PRAYER PROMPTS

1. How has your life been silenced?

2. What can you do now to reclaim your voice?

3. What can you do to accept and care for your mind and body?

4. Pray for physical and emotional healing.

CHAPTER FOUR

RAGE

*The child who is
not embraced by
the village will
burn it down to
feel its warmth.*

WEST AFRICAN PROVERB

In 2 Samuel we read of the rape of Tamar by her half-brother Amnon and the resulting devastation. Amnon pretends to be ill and manipulates King David to send Tamar to his bedroom with a meal to help him get well. Once she's inside the bedroom, Amnon rapes his sister, and then we read he "hated her with intense hatred. In fact, he hated her more than he had loved her." Amnon demands that Tamar, "Get up and get out!" Tamar's soul is so shattered that she believes she could actually stay with him. She tells Amnon, "Sending me away would be a greater wrong than what you have already done to me." Amnon publicly humiliates her by demanding that his personal servant "get this woman out of my sight and bolt the door after her." His servant puts Tamar out, and "Tamar put ashes on her head and tore the ornate robe she was wearing. She put her

hands on her head and went away, weeping aloud as she went"
(2 Samuel 13:15-19 NIV).

When Tamar's brother Absalom discovers what happened he
tells her, "Be quiet for now, my sister; he is your brother. Don't take
this thing to heart" (v. 20). Tamar was unable to process the abuse
or rid herself of the shame she felt, so she internalized it and emotionally collapsed. Tamar's rage turned inward and against herself,
and she lived in Absalom's house as a desolate woman never to
speak again of the horror. When King David discovered what happened, he was furious, yet he did nothing to bring about justice. In
the book of Romans there is a reminder: "Do not take revenge, my
dear friends, but leave room for God's wrath, for it is written: 'It is
mine to avenge; I will repay,' says the Lord" (Romans 12:19 NIV).
Absalom didn't wait for God or King David; he was determined to
bring justice for his sister. Though he never said a word to Amnon,
his rage simmered just below the surface—he spent two years
plotting revenge. After Absalom convinced King David to send
Amnon and the rest of the king's sons to meet him, Absalom ordered his men to kill Amnon and the rest of David's sons as they
tried to escape (2 Samuel 13:23-29). When we exact justice by any
means necessary, like Absalom, we believe we are God and can
judge and take vengeance rightly.

BITTER ROOT

In this story of Tamar, Absalom, Amnon, and King David, we can
see ourselves mirrored. African Americans and First Nations
members in this country were taken against our will. Black women,
men, and their kids were abused, discarded, and sold. Those generational scars and the current indignities affect us profoundly. In
Hebrews 12:15 we read, "See to it that no one fails to obtain the grace
of God; that no root of bitterness springs up and causes trouble, and
through it many become defiled." We may be bitter, blame ourselves,

take revenge, or imagine that somehow our abusers will be made to pay for what they did. This is not to say that reparations are not due, but holding onto and acting out of bitterness is like drinking poison and expecting the other person to die. The bitterness easily turns to rage.

Na'im Akbar, a clinical psychologist and author of *Chains and Images of Psychological Slavery*, shares how psychologists and sociologists have failed to recognize the far-reaching emotional and social impact slavery continues to have in the lives of African Americans.[1] Most African Americans are also unaware of the impact that pent up pain can have. Rage is one result.

Author Michelle Alexander writes, "Those of us who hope to be their allies should not be surprised, if and when this day comes, that when those who have been locked up and locked out finally have a chance to speak and truly be heard, and what we hear is rage."[2] Professor Kenneth V. Hardy writes, "Rage builds over time as a result of cumulative suppressed emotions precipitated by voicelessness." While we may get angry about a present situation, rage is a result of compounded assaults. Rage may present as deep sadness or explosive anger.[3] People of color are justifiably angry about the many injustices we face. The question is what to do with that anger before or after it turns to rage.

Carla and Caleb were never incarcerated, but there are ways that they have been locked up and locked out emotionally. In this chapter Caleb and Carla's stories illustrate how unprocessed and unhealed racial trauma easily turns into rage and how the Lord even meets us there.

CALEB

Caleb was an exception among his friends. He grew up with both parents in the home. His mom and dad were Christians, held good jobs, made a decent household income, and valued education.

Caleb and his friends didn't wake up one day and decide to be a gang, nor did they come together to terrorize the 'hood. They were just a circle of friends from the neighborhood who were tired of being marginalized and silenced. Caleb and his friends ran the streets, and eventually the line between homies from the 'hood and a gang was blurred. When the police opened a file officially labeling them as a gang, they became one by default. For Caleb, membership in the gang meant he now had a level of protection and covering, and he also accepted an unhealthy identity of what it is to be a Black man. He learned a distorted view of courage: to never back down no matter what. This is what makes you a man.

Meanwhile, Caleb excelled academically and passed the rigorous entrance exam into the prestigious Boston Latin High School. However, the racial bias and lack of academic support contributed to Caleb flunking out of school his first year. The next school year his only option was to attend a school in the 'hood. That school was the gateway to his drug and gang involvement. Part of Caleb's trauma story began with his experiences at that school.

The *Journal of Emotional Abuse* confirms racism's impact on the education of African American males. Racism "contributed to low teacher expectations, heavy reliance on biased standardized tests, the overrepresentation of African American males in special education, and the disproportionally large numbers of kids of color who are diagnosed with Attention Deficit Hyperactivity Disorder (ADHD) and placed on Ritalin."[4] The teachers at Caleb's school didn't seem to know what to do with the traumatized Black and Brown youth they were to educate. Their lesson plans were drained of creativity—they taught by route. The students were bored and easily agitated, which resulted in spontaneous fights between students and sometimes involved a teacher. In and around the school drug dealing was an open secret. The students were adrift without adult supervision and support during a pivotal time in their identity formation. Author Ralph Ellison wrote in *Invisible Man*, "I am an invisible man. . . . I am a man of substance, of flesh and bone, fiber and liquids—and I might even be said to possess a mind. I am invisible, understand, simply because people refuse to see me."[5]

Despite his supportive family, Caleb says, "My identity was mostly shaped by what I experienced in the streets, the media, propaganda, the negative aspects of hip-hop music, and false masculinity." Caleb didn't process what he saw in the media with his parents or his youth pastor; he simply ingested it whole. "Youth exposure to victimization is directly linked to negative outcomes for young people, including increased depression, substance abuse, risky sexual behavior, homelessness, and poor school performance."[6] Caleb's life soon revolved around the streets, partying, engaging in petty crime, and selling weed. Some of his friends sold harder drugs and were involved in violence, and for a time they all evaded incarceration.

Caleb and his friends witnessed someone get shot in a drive-by, and the next day they went to school as if nothing happened. One friend even joked about getting shot, but they never really talked about the trauma of what they saw or how they felt. In the early 2000s the city of Boston had one full-time youth worker. There was no one to walk alongside the inner-city youth to help them deal with their trauma. There were also no Black or Brown therapists, and the teens didn't trust the White therapists. One estimate finds that "only between two and fifteen percent of victims of all ages ever receive any victim assistance, and another indicates that among African American victims, only about nine percent of people sought help from non-police agencies that provided services."[7] Only years later did Caleb realize that not everyone had these kinds of experiences that seemed a normal part of life to him.

The community needed more Black police officers who understood and cared about the community. But the random stop-and-frisk policies of the police department caused teens like Caleb to distrust the police. The Center for Constitutional Rights reports that stop and frisks often have a "lasting emotional impact." The people interviewed "described feeling a range of emotions during stops, including anger, fear, shame, and vulnerability. One man described feeling 'disgusted, insulted, humiliated! And angry! Absolutely angry.'"[8] Because of the risk of being racially profiled, Caleb's life was mostly limited to a few square blocks. He and his crew would not go to other areas like communities on Cape Cod, Newton, or Brookline because they didn't want to feel uncomfortable or tailed by store security. They figured that if they did go, they might as well steal something, because that's what was expected of them.

Michelle Alexander writes, "When a young man who was born in the ghetto and who knows little of life beyond the walls of his prison cell and the invisible cage that has become his life, turns to us in bewilderment and rage, we should do nothing more than look him in the eye and tell him the truth."[9] The truth is that racism and systemic oppression set him up for trauma and death. Researchers Janet Currie and Erdal Tekin report that when a youth is victimized the likelihood of committing a violent or nonviolent crime increases.[10]

The only option for Caleb and his crew was to suck it up or stuff their anger. But this was soon followed by rage-fueled eruptions—threats and then violence against themselves and their community—attempting to prove their manhood. They were devalued, and they devalued each other in turn. As Caleb reflects back on his adolescence, he grieves for the friend he lost to suicide, another who is serving twenty-five years in jail for murder, and others who were stabbed or shot and survived yet still carry trauma. Caleb is angry: "I shouldn't have to be dealing with these kinds of life-and-death situations." Caleb needed help, but it was a long time coming.

CARLA

Carla grew up in the same community as Caleb. She is the eldest of two kids raised by a single mom. One day as she sat in a meeting quietly listening and yet somewhat distracted, the word *rage* was impressed upon her heart. It was utterly unrelated to what was being discussed in the meeting. Carla had no context for it and never thought of herself as an enraged person. However, since that moment she has taken an honest look at her racial trauma and rage: its origin, how it affects her behavior, how she manages and wants to be healed from it.

Carla's mom grew up in the Roxbury area; she and her family members were card-carrying members of the Wampanoags, a First Nation tribe in Massachusetts, and she also has an African American lineage. Reportedly the Wampanoag tribe was the first to greet the Pilgrims and celebrated the first Thanksgiving with them. Carla's grandmother worked each day cleaning the homes of Jewish families while Carla's mom attended school in the neighborhood. The school was an unsafe emotional and physical environment for Black and Brown kids. The Irish Catholic school teachers were harsh; the ruler was often used as an instrument of torture rather than teaching. Although there were upwardly mobile Black families who lived on Fort Hill with its stately Victorian homes, Carla's mom's family was poor. They struggled to put food on the table, and her mom carried a deep shame about being pegged as a second-class citizen. Carla's father grew up in Everett, Massachusetts, with both of his parents. They were working-class homeowners. A Vietnam veteran, he met Carla's mom after the war. His parents were not thrilled about the marriage. Soon Carla's parents were involved in a local chapter of the Black Panthers, and in their early twenties, Carla was born.

In 1974 when Carla was one year old, her dad went missing. For many years her mother made up some story about his passing. Carla would ask her aunts to tell her about her father because she understood on an unconscious level that her mother didn't really want to talk about him. Carla would say, "My mother said he was really sick and died on his way to the hospital in a cab." She saw the look in her aunt's eyes and heard conflicting things about his death. There was more to the story. Years later when Carla was ten years old, she asked her mother for the truth. Carla's mother said he was involved in community activism and he and his friend were pursued by the police. The neighbors reported that the last time they saw him, he was being chased. He and his friend never returned. Carla's mother waited, and the days turned to weeks. Then a month later both of their bodies turned up in a local river. She never got the details of which river, and no investigation was conducted. It was labeled an accident, and the case was closed. After finally hearing the true story, Carla sobbed for what seemed like hours and then she shut down her grief. To this day when Carla's mom talks about her husband, she dissolves into tears. She has never had any kind of therapy around this trauma.

Carla remembers asking her mom, "Why didn't you get any help?" and her mom said, "I was afraid that if I started talking and I cried I would never stop, I would be completely swallowed up, and I had a baby and decided that I wasn't going to go there." Over time Carla no longer had any real thoughts or questions about her dad. It was too painful, too ugly to look at, mainly because she couldn't process any of it with her mom.

Years later the pain resurfaced when she participated in an inner-healing support group. During that time Carla had her first boyfriend, and he was so much like her father. He too was 6 feet 5 inches and had to duck beneath the doorway to enter a room. Her new boyfriend wore dreadlocks; her dad had worn an afro—both were pro-Black statement hairdos of the day. During a group meeting Carla remembers a woman in her group saying, "Maybe you have been looking for your father all these years." One day while Carla and her mom were in a shop, a woman walked in and froze when she saw Carla's mom. The woman was the girlfriend of the man who drowned with Carla's father. After looking at each other for a while, Carla's mom and the woman embraced and wept as if their loss happened the day before. Carla's been processing things like this in therapy for years and has found a measure of healing.

But something happened to Carla after all of the viral videos of the shooting deaths of so many unarmed Black men. Carla has been triggered and struggled with rage and depression, and it began to affect her friendships. She's always looking over her shoulder and unsure if she can partner deeply with White folks. She's never had the personal experience of being targeted or marginalized by police officers; her interactions have been pretty positive. However, her fear of and anger at officers have something to do with what happened to her mom and dad. Carla fears that rage and grief may be a thorn in her side for the rest of her life. The rage and grief are two sides of the same coin. When she is feeling stuck in rage, she may be denying grief; and when she's stuck in grief, it is likely that anger needs to be addressed.

TRANSFORMATION

Absalom was stuck in rage against his father, and he acted upon it. He was so deeply grieved by the rape and humiliation of his sister that he tried to overthrow the king. The rebellion failed, and as

Absalom made his escape on a mule, his long hair got caught in a tree and he was killed (2 Samuel 18).

After Absalom's death, King David finally awoke to his deep grief. However, was his grief because of Absalom's death or because he felt guilty that the deaths of his sons may have been prevented if he had responded differently to the rape? We are like these biblical characters in several ways:

- We are like Tamar when we turn our rage inward and blame or shame ourselves, and soon our anger incapacitates us.

- We are like Absalom when we take revenge on those who hurt us.

- We are like David when we do nothing and deny how we feel only to have our anger come back later and bite us.

In Ephesians 4:25-27 we are instructed to put away falsehood and "speak the truth to our neighbors, for we are members of one another. Be angry but do not sin; do not let the sun go down on your anger, and do not make room for the devil." We are told to "put away from you all bitterness and wrath and anger and wrangling and slander, together with all malice, and be kind to one another, tenderhearted, forgiving one another, as God in Christ has forgiven you" (v. 31-32). How do we do this when we are enraged? Healing starts with the awareness that there is a problem. The journey of healing for Carla and Caleb is ongoing. There will be future injustices, and they will need to process and obtain freedom from their rage. As they surrender their rage to the Lord, it is transformed by faith and acts of service in the context of community, and they will find physical release.

Faith. Carla says she's had this ongoing struggle with the Lord; she feels outraged and confused, and too often her posture toward him is angry. She has asked, "Lord, where are you when someone's twelve-year-old baby is killed in broad daylight for the entire world to see and there's no recourse; his blood is simply spilled on the ground?" Carla says that one day while praying, she believes the Lord spoke strongly to her heart: "You're not going to make it if you're not on your knees praying on a daily basis." When Carla contemplates moving forward and navigating ongoing racism, she knows she needs to stay in this posture. This is where the Lord meets her in her grief and rage in a way that nothing and no one else can.

Caleb says his faith helps him to persevere; he goes to a church that lays out the gospel case for racial and social justice. The church leaders and members strive to allow the gospel to inform their response. The kids in the 'hood get more than just talk; they get to see that something is happening.

Acts of service. After graduating high school, Caleb's parents were part of a mission team planning to serve in Johannesburg, South Africa. The team would be attending a reconciliation conference and serving in an informal settlement. Caleb, his younger brother, Ethan, and two friends were invited to join the team. The team hoped that the trip would be as much a transformational time for the teens as it would be for those in need.

South Africa was a challenge from the start. The reconciliation conference was held in a somewhat dilapidated youth hostel and community center in Soweto. The conference attendees included Black, White, and Colored South Africans who shared their stories of life under apartheid, the former brutal system of institutionalized racial segregation and discrimination. As folks shared about the loss of loved ones, the oppression, and their hopes for racial reconciliation, everyone was emotionally moved except for Caleb and the other teens. When the team went to serve at Emthonjeni, an HIV/AIDS ministry, the teens' attitude began to change. Located in an old Dutch colonial farmhouse, Emthonjeni was situated in the middle of an informal settlement of over five thousand shacks without running water or proper sanitation.

The team painted the interior and exterior of the farmhouse and then followed dirt paths into the settlement and ministered to the kids, many of whom were affected by HIV/AIDS. The trip was a milestone for Caleb. This was the first overseas trip for him where he encountered people worse off than he was, yet they were resourceful and resilient. This was the first time he felt he was a blessing and not a social liability. He was surprised as people asked him to pray for them. It was also monumental because even though weed and alcohol were readily available in the settlement, this was the longest period of time that Caleb remained sober. So, when Nick, his older Black mentor, sat him down and told him if he didn't change his life he wasn't going to make it, he was finally able to hear it.

Kenneth V. Hardy reports, "Although suffering from internalized devaluation and an assaulted sense of self, there is an untapped hero within that has been overshadowed by stereotyping, pathologizing, demonizing, and criminalizing."[11] While in South Africa, Caleb and his crew served others well, and the hero in each one of them emerged. The trip to South Africa changed the trajectory of Caleb's life.

Community. Given our political and social climate, Carla sometimes feels like she's "sort of underwater" concerning the grief and rage. But her membership in a healthy, supportive, and woke church has been God's gift to her. Her relationship with people across the color lines has been profoundly healing. She has the freedom to express Black grief and rage. Some folks weep and mourn with her; others become angry with her at the injustice. She does have conflicts with her friends about race issues and privilege and the ways that these manifest in their relationship. But they also understand that they are going to remain committed to each other.

This has been powerful for Carla. When she and her friend Liza, a Latina, come together and talk about these things, Carla is blessed by her friend's profound, enriched historical understanding. So much of what Liza does is a lament; she cries out to God, which is powerful intercession that ushers in healing.

Caleb eventually graduated college. At his first job he didn't feel he fit in and didn't understand the White culture. When incidents of racism occurred, the Whites talked among themselves; no one came to him. He felt so alone that he had to parse his words so they would not be picked apart. Sometimes Caleb had to get louder to be heard, and instead of reaching for reconciliation, in anger he reached for the opposite. He knows White folks may never understand what his community is going through, but the Lord can take his anger and transform it. Caleb now works at a Christian ministry where people of color and White folks talk truth to power, and the leadership accepts critique.

Caleb wants Christian churches, organizations, and communities to be more diverse. When he performs Christian hip-hop at churches in the city or suburbs, he notices few have urban millennials of color. His friends joke about their perception of the church. They want no part of the White evangelical Jesus. Caleb wants to change that. He says that "the gospel does not have to look so foreign to Black and Brown folks." He sees the need for churches where elders embrace change and invest in the youth; where instruction, support, and encouragement are taken seriously; and where the gospel is contextualized to meet the reality of life in the inner city.

Physical release. A church in Roxbury is removing the stigma from mental illness and getting help with grief and trauma. The church founded the Cory Johnson Program for Post-Traumatic healing, which deals with trauma holistically. They host an open mic night where all are welcome to share their story or whatever is on their heart, and there's time to write and journal. Carla feels safe there. It's been a space and time of connection that has helped her to deal with the racial trauma that she still carries in her body. She's participated in the trauma-informed yoga exercises that encourage destressing. Carla was struck by the immediate release; she could immediately feel her body react. She came into one session feeling tired and stressed, but it soon melted away, which she is grateful for. Carla also releases her rage through personal and corporate worship. During worship God accesses different parts of her heart and her brain. When she is singing, she also feels all sensation of heaviness falling away. She remembers in South Africa the church folks would dance in the Holy Spirit. It wasn't the kind of liturgical dance where things were happening up front, but everyone was free, dancing and singing in the aisle, almost like a dance party. Carla says there is healing that comes when she also engages the Lord with her body in this way.

For Caleb music has been a vehicle to release pent-up grief and anger. He is careful about how much negativity he takes in through music and the media, even the social justice videos that aim to leave him enraged. He is aware that some stories are recycled to get folks fired up. He doesn't deny that racism and microaggression are real, but he also reads, watches, and listens to the good stuff about what God is doing and where reconciliation and social justice are happening. This prevents hopelessness and the lie that God is not at work.

Although we may wonder if Jesus prioritizes love and justice, he does. He says there are consequences for those who ignore and abuse the poor and marginalized. In Matthew 25:44-45 Jesus says, "Then they also will answer, 'Lord, when was it that we saw you hungry or thirsty or a stranger or naked or sick or in prison, and did not take care of you?' Then he will answer them, 'Truly I tell you, just as you did not do it to one of the least of these, you did not do it to me.'" When we experience racial trauma and injustice, we need help to not turn our anger inward and then outward in self-destructive rage. The Lord is familiar with our trauma, so we can submit our anger to the Lord and confide in others we trust before and after it turns to rage. As we do this, we discover that our anger and rage can be transformed and used constructively as fuel for positive change.

REFLECTION AND PRAYER PROMPTS

1. Are you struggling with anger or rage? If so, why and how is it expressed?

2. What are some things that can help you to process your anger or rage?

3. How might the Lord be calling you to harness your anger for your benefit and that of others?

CHAPTER FIVE

FEAR

I learned that courage was not the absence of fear,
but the triumph over it.

Nelson Mandela, *Long Walk to Freedom*

A White police officer in Ferguson, Missouri, confronted teenager Michael Brown as he walked down the middle of Canfield Drive. There are conflicting reports, but after the encounter Michael Brown lay dead in the street with six bullet wounds. It was a hot August day, and Michael's body was left on the road for four and a half hours.

The message sent to the Black community was no different than the one sent by the lynching of Black folks in this country before, during, and after emancipation. It's the same message that Rome sent when Jesus was flogged with a cat o' nine tails, made to carry his cross through the streets, and crucified on Calvary for all to see. The Romans wanted to stop a movement and quell any potential rebellion. The message sent to the followers of Jesus and to communities of color is simple: cease, desist, and obey, or crucifixion or lynching will be your fate.

Bryan Stevenson, author of *Just Mercy*, writes, "Racial terror lynching was a tool used to enforce Jim Crow laws and racial segregation—a tactic for maintaining racial control by victimizing the entire African American community, not merely punishment of an alleged perpetrator for a crime."[1] It's estimated that about two hundred households had a full view of Michael as he laid in the street.

That day in Ferguson the entire community was racially traumatized and victimized. Black parents tried to shield their kids from the grisly scene but were unable to avert their own eyes. They were unable to erase from their minds the sight of somebody's child left in the street like roadkill. There were official excuses and protestations about why Michael's body laid in the street for hours. But the message to the Black community, whether intentional or not, was that Black lives do not matter. Brutal actions like lynching, Michael Brown lying in the street, and Christ's crucifixion serve the same purpose for those in power—to instill fear and terror.

A FEAR-BASED MESSAGE

Across the United States systemic racism now has a bullhorn that sends the same fear-stoking message. The message also tells people of color that our inclusion is conditional. The message includes:

- Be afraid, because you will never be welcomed here.

- Okay, your women and kids can come, but not the men. They are too scary.

- No, you're not welcome, because we're afraid there are too many of you.

- Yes, you can come, but what you need to succeed will be blocked or withheld because you want to replace us.

Almost every day on social media a video depicting racism, microaggression, and racial profiling emerges prompted by the actions of another "concerned" White citizen. A manager at a Starbucks called the police on two Black men sitting in the restaurant waiting for a friend. A college tour turns ugly after a woman called the campus police because two First Nation teenagers on tour made her "uneasy." Other videos show White privilege in action. In Oakland, California, a White woman called the police because a Black family was barbecuing in the park. In New York, a White attorney erupted in a racist tirade upon hearing café staff talking to customers in Spanish. The list goes on. These experiences carry a message that people of color are not welcome and are in danger in majority White spaces. These racist incidents harken back to the removal of indigenous people, racist Black codes and Jim Crow laws, and the Chinese Exclusion Act of the past. These laws were enacted to segregate, police, and regulate the bodies and behavior of people of color.

It has been said that the opposite of love is fear. When people of color are marginalized and face hatred instead of love, the fruit is fear. Fear and anxiety are a byproduct of racial trauma. When fear enters, love and compassion flee. Feelings of fear and anxiety may or may not be rooted in an actual threat, and they range from mild to severe. The emotional symptoms of fear include nagging thoughts about potential threats, which become anxiety when they fill our minds and keep us from feeling present in our bodies and fully engaged in life. Physical symptoms may include a racing heart, insomnia, shallow breathing, clammy hands, headaches, and muscle aches.

This chapter features Kanti, a First Nation woman, and Jonathan, an African American millennial. The racism and racial trauma experienced by Kanti and Jonathan have some historical similarities but are different; so are the ways they experienced fear and anxiety. Kanti's fear is rooted in and connected to the cultural genocide of her people. Jonathan's fear is related to concerns for his physical safety and that of other people of color.

KANTI

The questions of home, identity, and fear are central to the story of Kanti, a Shinnecock, Cherokee, and African American woman. The name Kanti means "sing" in English. Kanti is proud of who she is, yet for much of her life she struggled with which group she belonged to. When her family moved from the Shinnecock Reservation to a mostly Black community in Philadelphia, she experienced colorism because of her light complexion. She was often questioned about why she was so light skinned and why her hair was so straight. At her grammar school there wasn't a real understanding or teaching about what it meant to be First Nation. Kanti remembers during first grade her teacher made her stand in front of the class to talk about First Nation culture and what life was like on the reservation. Kanti was quite shy, but she spoke with a smile as she shared how they made fry bread and succotash, the First Nation rituals, and the annual powwow. She shared memories of how she spends every summer on the reservation near the Peconic Bay just a few steps away from where her aunties and cousins live, and the days spent clamming and later selling the clams in town. She'd make beads called wampompeag (wampum) from the purplish inside of the clam shells. Wampompeag was traditionally used by the Shinnecock and many other Northeast tribes as currency; now it's used to make beautiful jewelry. The experience of sharing her heritage was empowering for Kanti, yet in other ways it further isolated her from her peers at the mostly Black grammar school.

Kanti still struggles with her mixed heritage as people try to pigeonhole her race and ethnicity. But she feels at her current age she has to be okay with being three-fourths First Nation and one quarter African American. Many years ago, to become an officially recognized member of the Shinnecock Nation, Kanti went through a process of verifying her lineage. The name Shinnecock means "people of the stony shore." For thousands of years the tribe lived on their ancestral land, thousands of acres of pristine land on the Shinnecock Bay. The Shinnecock valued their history and land and prioritized the tribe rather than the individual. However, their communal life was disrupted when the White settlers arrived. Like many other First Nation tribes, the settlers hatched a plan to remove the Shinnecock from their land.

Author Francis Jennings outlines the systematic way the First Nation land was stolen.[2] The White settlers would appoint a First Nation chief and give him authority over tribes in the area to sign away their land. They introduced alcohol to the tribe, which resulted in alcoholism. This was followed by the breakdown of cultural values of community and honoring the land. The White settlers encouraged the invasion of First Nation land. Boundary lines were tested as settlers built near this land and let their live-stock destroy First Nation crops. The Whites used outside statutes and ordinances to compromise local tribal autonomy and used law enforcement for any infraction—from individual acts of violence to engaging in traditional religious ceremonies.

Kanti's words carry traces of anger, fear, and sadness as she relays how the Shinnecock land was taken. In 1859, the White residents on Long Island drafted an agreement in which the Shinnecock were to transfer to them the right, title, and interest to their 3,600 acres. The Shinnecock leaders refused to sign. The White residents simply forged the signatures of the tribal leaders and filed the document of the transfer of property. The transfer was illegally granted by the state legislature, although only the US Congress is allowed to do this. At the time the Shinnecock objected, but with no legal recourse, the tribe was left with only eight hundred acres of their ancestral land. There are now over fourteen hundred members of the Shinnecock nation. Over seven hundred live on the reservation; Kanti and the rest live elsewhere.

In 2005 the Shinnecock sued the government to recover their stolen land, which includes the famous Shinnecock Hills Golf Club—believed to be the location of their ancestral burial grounds. The Shinnecock lost the case in 2006 because the presiding judge ruled "there has been a 'dramatic change' in the demographics of the area and the character of the property."[3] Any sort of land transfer would therefore be prohibitively "disruptive." The Shinnecock filed an appeal and waited for the case to be heard. In the meantime, in October 2010 after a thirty-two-year battle that included suing the Department of the Interior, the Shinnecock were finally federally recognized by the US government as a First Nation tribe.

After ten years of waiting, in 2016 the US Court of Appeals in Manhattan upheld the ruling of 2006, and the US Supreme Court declined to review the decision without explanation.

The loss of the case was a devastating blow for the Shinnecock Nation. For Kanti, losing the suit is symptomatic of the historical racial trauma and barriers that have a direct consequence on her life and her community. Although many Shinnecock seem to carry on with life unaffected, below the surface, racial trauma, emotional pain, and fear remain. During the 2018 US Open Golf Championship, members of the Shinnecock Nation, some of Kanti's relatives, and their allies carried protest signs with slogans such as, "Stolen land, stolen name, stolen image, silenced voices never!" and "We are the voices of our ancestors." As they picketed in front of the Shinnecock Hills Golf Club, motorists along Montauk Highway honked their horns in solidarity.[4]

Kanti sees how her history and fear have affected all aspects of her life and her tribe. She realizes that fear, debt, poverty, and limited success and progress are not new things. They are echoes of words that have been spoken over First Nation people for generations. Kanti believes the infighting on the reservation and between First

Nation tribes is instigated by racist White people and the government: "They love it when we fight against each other." Another tactic to disrupt the First Nations has been an uptick in the availability of alcohol and drugs coming from the outside. The tribal council is intervening and getting people into treatment for their addictions. Kanti fears that unless they combat past and ongoing systemic racism and heal from racial trauma, it will result in the elimination of their language, cultural awareness, and pride.

JONATHAN

Jonathan lived in South Africa for nine years and only visited the United States three times during that period. Before moving back to attend college, his dad sat him down and gave him the talk that many African American males receive at some point in their lives. His dad told him about the racism he may face, how to engage with police, and what it means to be a Black man in the United States. Jonathan was encouraged to do the best he could and to not let anyone tell him he is less than anyone else or that he doesn't deserve to be in a particular place or have a specific job.

Most importantly he was reminded that he is a child of God. The talk helped him deal with the bias he soon faced when he and his dad visited the States to tour prospective colleges. When their flight landed, they were separated. Jonathan went through the US Customs checkpoint, his documents were examined, and he was allowed to enter. He arrived at the luggage carousel to await the delivery of his luggage when he was approached and detained by an airport officer. The officer looked him up and down and said, "I wanna see your passport." Jonathan's behavior was not out of line before, during, or after the flight. He wondered, *Is this because I am African American, arrived from South Africa, and have light-brown skin? Or maybe he thinks I'm Latino, undocumented, or a Muslim.* Jonathan complied, and the officer closely examined his photo and then slowly read each passport page. Rather curtly he asked Jonathan a string of questions, "Where are you coming from? What are your plans? What is the reason for being in the country? How long will you be staying?" The incident was unnerving and a bit demoralizing to Jonathan. Did onlookers think he was a criminal or undocumented? The officer never stated why he detained Jonathan or asked those questions. Nor did he interrogate any of the White arrivals. He simply handed the passport back to Jonathan and walked away without a word.

In 2012 the *New York Times* reported that the Transportation Security Administration officials received written complaints from thirty-two officers about racial profiling occurring at Boston's Logan Airport. The officers said that the managers demanded high numbers of stops, searches, and criminal referrals. This led to targeting minorities with the hope that those stops would lead to outstanding arrest warrants or immigration problems. The report brought to light the need to examine how airports across the country might also be engaging in racial profiling.[5] Some may view Jonathan's experience as a minor inconvenience, but this racial profiling is one of many incidents of microaggression that he and other people of color face.

These incidents were internalized by Jonathan and later resurfaced as anger, cynicism, and negativity. They affected his sleep, but mostly he battled fear. Jonathan says that the airport incident revealed that "I couldn't just step back into my old life. It was long gone." Boston is home, but he was now entering into an entirely new reality and culture.

Jonathan had to make the adjustment that many third-culture kids do when they return to the place of their birth or their parents' home country. The place once thought of as home is now not entirely home, or it is not what he thought it should be. This was a bit frightening for Jonathan. However, he was determined to return to the United States for college the next year. In July 2014, he packed as many of his belongings as he could fit into two suitcases (including his anxiety), and he boarded a plane for Boston. One thing about fear is that it can keep us in hiding and in lockdown. We can become like the disciples who dispersed after Jesus' arrest, trial, and crucifixion. They were so terrorized and traumatized by Jesus' death that they hid in fear. One disciple, John, remained near to Jesus during this time. But Peter, who Jesus had foretold would deny him, actually refused to acknowledge he even knew the Lord.

Jonathan spent much of the first semester of his freshman year in hiding as he battled fear, anxiety, and hypervigilance. He remained on campus and used studying as an excuse and a way of escape, spending hours in his dorm room or in the library to avoid what was happening around the country. Things began to shift late in his first semester after he joined the Black Student Union and the multicultural office at his college. The other shift happened when he took a class where his reading assignments linked the themes in the book to the fear that society has always had regarding Black males. The class challenged and energized Jonathan to leave the place of fear and hiding. He took a risk and participated in a march organized by the Black Student Unions of several area colleges. A diverse group of students gathered on that cold day and marched through the streets of the Fenway. It was partly in response to a grand jury's failure to indict the police officers who had choked Eric Garner to death and the officer who shot Michael Brown. Jonathan also protested his college administration's failure to create a safe and affirming environment for students of color.

During the spring semester, Jonathan attended the InterVarsity Black Campus Ministries conference, which was attended by hundreds of students of color and a few White allies. It was a safe place for him to open up, learn, share, and pray about his struggles as a young Black man in the United States. Reading from the book of Isaiah, he was reminded, "Do not fear, for I have redeemed you; I have called you by name, you are mine" (Isaiah 43:1). The conference was an important reminder that God loves and cares for him. The theme of the conference was from the book of Revelation: "After this I looked, and there before me was a great multitude that no one could count, from every nation, tribe, people and language, standing before the throne and before the Lamb" (Revelation 7:9 NIV). This verse was an encouragement to fully embrace his Christian and racial identity.

THE ONGOING JOURNEY OUT OF FEAR

During the crucifixion of Christ, a few courageous female disciples refused to bow down to fear. They remained in the crowd as silent witnesses praying for Jesus. Those women risked it all because of his great love for them and their great love for him. Later at the tomb they found the stone rolled away and the tomb empty.

Maybe the women were able to push past their fears because they encouraged one another to do so. Because they did it, they were blessed to be among the first to see that Jesus had risen. Mary Magdalene had a powerful encounter with Jesus, who told her to go to where the disciples were hiding and tell them that Jesus had risen. Later that night Jesus entered that room and proclaimed, "Peace be with you." He showed them the wounds on his hands and side. He said to the disciples, "As the Father has sent me, so I send you." Then he breathed on them and said, "Receive the Holy Spirit" (John 20:21-22). This same Jesus loves us so much that he's given us the Holy Spirit, the Comforter, to help us address our fears and heal our pervasive anxiety. The American poet laureate Maya Angelou wrote, "Hope and fear cannot occupy the same space at the same time. Invite one to stay."[6] Sometimes the Lord helps us to become and stay free with the help of others like a good therapist or a support group, and if our fear is debilitating, this may include good medication.

The night after the 2016 presidential election Jonathan went to work at his volunteer position at a youth writing and publishing organization. He tutors students in writing and offers help with their homework. He was already emotionally exhausted from the election when he was paired with a ten-year-old girl born in Mexico. When he asked how she was doing, her eyes filled with tears as she confided, "I am scared. My parents don't have their papers. They might be deported now that Trump is president." Jonathan tried to reassure her that the government had checks and balances. But he could see that nothing he said helped her to feel better. He also felt dishonest because he didn't know what would really happen under the new administration. He had no right to give her any assurances.

As Jonathan walked home that evening he was both sad and angry about how the peace and joy of this innocent child had been stolen. He walked and prayed prayers of lament, which offered some solace. He found encouragement from the words written in Proverbs 31:8-9:

> Speak out for those who cannot speak,
> > for the rights of all the destitute.
> Speak out, judge righteously,
> > defend the rights of the poor and needy.

He believes this word was not only for him but also for the church and the world. However, after the inauguration, the threats of deportations grew, and the Deferred Action for Childhood Arrivals program for those who were brought into the country as children (Dreamers) was in jeopardy. Jonathan participated in a rally on Boston Common to protect the rights of the Dreamers. He continued to pray for the vulnerable kids in his program and their parents. Two years after the election folks still weren't settling well into this new normal. For some it's a strange new world, and for many others it's all too familiar.

When Jonathan read on Twitter about the White supremacist rally at the University of Virginia and what happened to Heather Heyer, it pushed him over the edge. Once again, Jonathan battled with anxiety in majority-White spaces and in the proximity of law enforcement. He believes the racist and anti-Semitic slurs are a consequence of the political and social rhetoric welcomed and unleashed under the current president. It was taking the country back to a time when America was never great for Black and Brown people.

TRANSCENDING RACIAL TRAUMA AND FEAR

Many First Nation Christians have also embraced the vision from the book of Revelation. They see their people standing around the throne of God with palm branches in their hands and praising God in their mother tongues. There is a place for the Shinnecock there, and it is by God's grace that the Shinnecock are still standing here. They are a sovereign nation within this country, refusing to let their way of life die. Sometimes life on the reservation can be difficult, yet the Lord loves and saves these resilient people. The Presbyterian church is an integral part of life on the reservation. During the summers Kanti attends the church and actively serves where she is needed. On matters of First Nation Christian faith Kanti says, "As young Christians we were told that the First Nation faith and rituals were taboo, but now Christians are integrating their faith with their rich culture." Kanti longs for more of the Shinnecock language and culture to be included in the Presbyterian worship services on the reservation.

They are not engaging in syncretism, practicing their traditional religion alongside Christianity, but they are looking at their

First Nation culture and religion and finding where the Creator, Jesus, and the Spirit have been there all along. They read the Scriptures in their mother tongue and have incorporated traditional drums into worship.[7] Megan Murdock Krischke, who helped launch and grow Native InterVarsity, says, "There are quite a few Native traditional values that are biblical." She shared how First Nation tribes respond with generosity and hospitality like the early church in the book of Acts. They also value family and relationships over accomplishments. One interesting difference in Christian First Nation churches, she says, is that the worship songs are more petitionary and the focus of prayer is oriented toward praise and adoration. Unlike the more Eurocentric approach, there's an oral and storytelling way of doing Scripture study. Megan observes, "There are a lot of things non-Native Christians could learn from Native culture."[8]

Kanti says, "I cope with racism and racial trauma by going to the reservation and talking with my family, my cousins, and my ninety-year-old aunt. I get away from the outside world, and any trauma that we have is talked about in a group. We help each other deal with those outside influences." Kanti spoke of how circles are important to the Shinnecock. The circle is symbolic; it has no end: "We do a lot of things in circle." It represents the never-ending connection she has with God and the interconnectedness between the members of the Shinnecock Nation. This connection was evident to Kanti when her husband passed away several years ago and her dearest cousin dropped everything and sped to Philadelphia to be by her side. The tribe also rallied around her. The circle also represents interconnectedness between First Nation tribes. The annual powwow is a gathering of tribes united on the circle. The Shinnecock powwow is held on a raised circle or mound where the different sovereign nations—dressed in stunning indigenous attire—present traditional drumming and dancing.

Below the circle are the observers. Apart from the pageantry the powwow is a time for the nations to come together and feast, exchange ideas, and strategize about how to make things better for First Nation peoples.

As recent as the 1970s the children of First Nation tribes were placed into boarding schools and attended public schools where their language was not taught or spoken. The result is that many of the preceding generation are unable to speak the language. Kanti is delighted that the Shinnecock are now reclaiming their language. The Shinnecock now have a school on the reservation where a whole unit is devoted to their language; even the little ones in preschool are learning to speak it. Kanti is eager to move back onto the reservation, but space is limited, so she will have to wait for someone to pass on in order to get a piece of land. She is willing to wait. For now she spends as much time on the reservation as she can and contributes where she can. She feels hopeful as she sees some of the young people taking a stand for the tribe.

Attorneys, other professionals, and working people still live on the reservation. Others work hard on the outside, and some who left the reservation for college have returned. Kanti says, "It's important for the young ones to see them return and stay." Recently there have been other hopeful signs that the town of Southampton is honoring the Shinnecock culture and tradition. A builder found bones on a development site that clearly is part of the Shinnecock burial grounds. The town paid the developers for the land and returned it to the Shinnecock.[9] The Shinnecock are still awaiting the final word on litigation about their stolen land and fishing rights. Perhaps the town and the country will finally do the right thing.

Jonathan has been able to deal with fear, as Audre Lorde's famous quote states, "Caring for myself is not self-indulgence, it is self-preservation, and that is an act of political warfare."[10] Jonathan has found that prioritizing the care of his soul has been a major contributor to stress relief. His soul is fed through reading Bible verses such as Philippians 4:6-7: "Do not worry about anything, but in everything by prayer and supplication with thanksgiving let your requests be made known to God. And the peace of God, which surpasses all understanding, will guard your hearts and your minds in Christ Jesus." Jonathan senses God's peace, and the fear for his physical safety recedes. The same is true when he spends time praying, listening to worship music, hanging out with friends, and riding his bike. He is a prolific writer of poetry and prose, pouring his heart out on paper. He also engages in activism, attends protests, organizes, and votes. Jonathan is hopeful with the recent appointment of Boston's forty-fifth police commissioner, the first person of color to hold that position. It means a lot to Jonathan and the community that the new commissioner was sworn into office at an African American church in the 'hood. Jonathan's activism has helped alleviate his fears and anxiety. He no longer feels that change will never happen or that he is powerless; he now believes change is possible.

The fear that Jonathan and Kanti carried was not totally unfounded. The same is true for us, and in light of this we must determine to live unbound from fear. We likely will enter spaces and have encounters in the future that are explicitly or subversively unwelcoming or hostile. The question is how will we respond? It is wise to be aware yet refuse to obsess with worry: *Am I going to be accepted or will I be treated unfairly?* When there is another racist incident and fear rears its ugly head, we can remember God's assurance of strength, comfort, love, and grace to help us manage, overcome fear, and confront whatever comes our way. There is also strength in numbers when people of color show up en masse. It sends a message that we will not cower in fear and anxiety. Whether in a group or alone, we have a God-given right to be there, and we can assert that right.

REFLECTION AND PRAYER PROMPTS

1. How have fear and anxiety affected your life?

2. What kind of support or activity do you think will help when your fear or anxiety is triggered? Make a list and post it where you can see it.

3. Ask the Lord for his perfect love to cast out fear and to fill you with peace.

CHAPTER SIX

LAMENT

*No one ever told me that grief felt so like fear. . . . The same
fluttering in the stomach, the same restlessness, and the yawning.
I keep on swallowing. At other times it feels like being mildly
drunk or concussed. There is a sort of invisible blanket
between the world and me.*

C. S. LEWIS, *A GRIEF OBSERVED*

In spring 2018, an order issued by the federal government mandated the separation of kids from their parents as they crossed into the United States from Mexico. I listened to a recording of a traumatized seven-year-old Guatemalan boy. The boy crossed the border with his father, and they were separated by US Immigration and Customs Enforcement. The Office of Refugee Resettlement detained the father and placed the boy in a shelter. They hadn't spoken in over a month. A devastating video recording of a phone call between the boy and his mama, still in Guatemala, emerged. The boy sobs as his mama tells him to "remember that God exists, honey, kneel and pray to God. Ask him to help you get out of there."

Her son responds, "Every time I go to sleep, I pray for you."

Mama tells her son, "God will help you. Take care of yourself. Don't cry, baby. Be happy. Go with God, baby." Her son responds, "Si, si, Mama."[1]

As we listened to the cries of the child and the faith of his mama, so many of our hearts broke. The public outcry over family separations like this came from all fronts, from the far left to the far right politically. The words written in the book of Lamentations 2:11 capture how many felt:

> My eyes are spent with weeping;
>   my stomach churns;
> my bile is poured out on the ground
>   because of the destruction of my people,
> because infants and babes faint
>   in the streets of the city.

It seems that anyone with a heart for children was enraged, and those with a history of childhood trauma were emotionally triggered. This injustice led to a groundswell of folks loudly proclaiming, "This is not America."

But it is America.

We have a history of this type of racially traumatizing behavior toward the most vulnerable. Enslaved families were routinely separated and sold off. First Nation children as young as five were taken from their parents and placed in government-run boarding schools. And Japanese families were detained in government internment camps. People of color live in the perpetual nightmare of racial trauma. We've prayed about it, but the answer is delayed for months, years, and decades.

THE CRY OF LAMENT

In 2 Samuel 21 we read about the lament of Rizpah, a traumatized mother grieved by an act of vengeance. King David handed her children over to the Gibeonites, who brutally murdered them and exposed their bodies on a hill. By law, they should have had a proper burial, but it was not allowed. Instead of leaving powerless, Rizpah took sackcloth, a sign of mourning, and spread it out on a rock near the place where her children were slain. There she sat from the beginning of the barley harvest until the rain poured down on the bodies. Rizpah sat in the scorching heat of day and the cold darkness of night. Each day she used her voice and head covering to scare away vultures. At night she was terrorized by howling jackals and wild animals lingering in the shadows. She kept watching. She waited. She wailed. She was a witness who refused to be moved.

Rizpah insisted that the king see her grief and acknowledge her pain and her cry for mercy and justice. This is the heart cry of those of us who carry unresolved grief that is as deep and wide as Rizpah's. We sit in that place of pain until God hears and answers. Sometimes we are consciously aware, and other times it's several years later before we discover that our losses are like those of Rizpah, and we have refused to move on.

Lament is described by Professor Soong-Chan Rah as "an act of protest as the lamenter is allowed to express indignation and even outrage about the experience of suffering. The lamenter talks back to God and ultimately petitions him for help, in the midst of pain. The one who laments can call out to God for help, and in that outcry, there is the hope and even the manifestation of praise."[2] Emmanuel Katongole "conceives of lament as 'a complex set of practices or disciplines—a way of *seeing, standing,* and *wrestling or arguing with* God, and thus a way of hoping in the midst of ruins.'"[3] The prayer of lament requires that we no longer hide or deny our racial trauma and pain. This type of prayer may take different forms: we may weep, complain, or scream; all can help expose how we truly feel. One prayer of lament is found in Psalm 44:24-26, which asks God:

> Why do you hide your face?
> Why do you forget our affliction and oppression?
> For we sink down to the dust;
> our bodies cling to the ground.
> Rise up, come to our help.
> Redeem us for the sake of your steadfast love.

King David's prayer of lament serves as an example of how, when faced with racism and injustice, we can also cry out to God. In prayer we begin by asking our God and King to listen to our words and consider our lament. We then remember and affirm his character and that he fights for us. We confess any confusion we may have about him. We vulnerably share our feelings about our abuse and abusers, and we ask for justice and healing. We praise him for his faithfulness and promise that he hears our prayers and answers them.

COMPOUNDED GRIEF

People of color cry out:

> How long must I bear pain in my soul,
> and have sorrow in my heart all day long?
> How long shall my enemy be exalted over me? (Psalm 13:2)

Glenn Schiraldi writes, "In trauma, we don't only lose something, we also lose our way. Hard-earned gains and dreams for the future seem irrevocably lost. Development is seriously impaired. Grieving is about finding our way again."[4] People of color have difficulty finding our way because our racial trauma has gone unprocessed and is ongoing, and now we have multiple losses and compounded grief. Mimi Abramovitz and Jochen Albrecht identified several "unpredictable and uncontrollable" losses experienced by people of color, each capable of producing extreme stress. "In conjunction with each other, the compounded impact results in serious prob-lematic consequences for both individuals and communities."[5] These compounded losses include the loss of a household member to foster care, incarceration, long-term hospitalization, or untimely death. Additionally, there is a loss of financial assets because of unemployment, job loss, foreclosure, or loss of home.[6] Many people of color live with decreased physical, psychological, and relational health; reduced access to employment, housing, and education; and adverse cognitive-emotional processing and quality of life because of unprocessed and compounded grief.[7]

The telltale symptoms of compounded or complicated grief are denial, low self-esteem, depression, anxiety, preoccupation with anger and rage, ambivalence, unresolved guilt, or shame about the significance of the trauma.[8] The journey of healing from racial trauma involves processing and grieving our compounded losses in a way that is not linear; there are no fixed stages—it's more like moving through a figure eight. We may repeatedly cycle through grief and then at some point we're able to live with the loss without it overtaking us.

Liza is an almost second-generation immigrant from Colombia, and Unathi is a South African millennial. They have lived with the complexities of unprocessed and compounded grief and are now experiencing healing through lament.

LIZA

The day after the presidential election, something changed in Liza. She went to work and was to lead a staff meeting; instead, she told the staff, "We're not going to do a staff meeting. We're just going to sit and cry." So they sat, and she played a worship song. The meeting was difficult for Liza, because she was one of only three people in visible distress; the rest were silent and seemed to be unmoved. Liza did not ask those in the room how they were feeling, but she realized how emotional health and community openness are prevented when Christians are taught to wear a smile all the time—even if it is a mask. How can we help each other understand that tears are appropriate? Tears don't mean you're emotionally unhinged. Tears and lament are healthy and healing.

Over a year later, as Liza sat in her car and listened to reports of the separation of refugee and immigrant children from their parents, she became overwhelmed with grief, anger, and fear. She was blindsided by her pain. She used her jacket to muffle the sounds of her sobs. It felt like 1994 when Proposition 187 passed in California. The proposition established a state-run citizenship screening system that prohibited undocumented immigrants from accessing essential health care services and public education. At that time Liza and her mom weren't naturalized, and she could hear the panic in her mom's voice as she said, "We gotta get our papers in order! We need to get naturalized right away before they start kicking Latinos out of this country."

Proposition 187 was followed by Proposition 209 in 1996, which put an end to affirmative action at governmental institutions, and in 1998 Proposition 227 limited bilingual education in public schools. It's almost twenty-five years later, and asylum seekers are literally fleeing for their lives from a country where the United States is complicit in its downturn. Yet many in the United States and the church want to turn the refugees away at the border. The road to the southern border is treacherous. Research has found that "although Hispanic families are more likely to experience traumatic immigration-related events that aren't often screened for, such as violence in one's home country, they are also less likely to seek mental health services than other groups."[9] Dr. Susana Rivera reports that immigrant families live in the shadows and carry inordinate stress and are isolated because "they fear being stopped by Immigration and Customs Enforcement (ICE). So they limit how often they leave their house, cramming all their errands and appointments for all family members into one day."[10] In a survey conducted from January 26 to April 9, 2017, one-third of Latinos and Latinas folks reported experiencing racial or ethnic slurs, being discriminated against when applying for jobs, and not being paid equally or considered for promotions. Thirty-one percent reported discrimination in housing, 27 percent said they have been personally discriminated against when interacting with police, and one in five said they have experienced violence or threats.[11] Perhaps Liza's mom was right that there was and is a concerted effort to block her people from immigration and integration into life in the United States.

UNATHI

In many ways the racial climate in postapartheid South Africa has changed dramatically for the better, but racism is still as rife there as it is in America. Each day Unathi witnessed the hold that White supremacy still had in the country. She saw White shopkeepers belittling Black South Africans, and at times she experienced the same. Unathi saw the fear and resignation in the eyes of a person falsely accused of shoplifting. She noticed that because of fear the person remained silent, unable to offer a defense. At times Unathi also remained silent. For Unathi anti-apartheid work meant first dealing with her own mind. She had to look at how she felt about herself and the grief that was holding her back from discerning the way forward. Unathi realized that no matter how many dreams she had or how ambitious she was, she faced barriers. These historical barriers had a direct consequence on her life and community. She was born in Mthatha, the capital city of the former Transkei in the Eastern Cape of South Africa.

The Transkei government was an English colony while the rest of the country was taken over by the Afrikaners. The English gave Black folks rights to own businesses: the offices, shops, restaurants, and hair salons created some thriving Black communities. Yet the rules of engagement were the same as for the rest of the country—mixing of the races was prohibited, people of color had to always carry an identity passbook, and freedom of movement was restricted by law. In Unathi's family, her grandmother was a nurse, and her grandfather a chartered accountant, but they were still considered inferior to the White minority.

In 1990, the world celebrated Nelson Mandela's release from prison after serving twenty-seven years for anti-apartheid activism. In 1994 apartheid fell, and after a surprisingly nonviolent election Nelson Mandela became South Africa's first Black president. The change in the country was dramatic. As restrictions were lifted Black folks became mobile, and many moved to bigger cities like Johannesburg thinking they'd have an even better life. Several businesses in Mthatha did not survive because people and monies left; some neighborhoods deteriorated. Some fathers were away at the mines, which created a fatherless generation.

Before Unathi's granddad died, he wouldn't sleep. He feared he would die, and his family wouldn't be provided for. He was right to be concerned. After he passed away the family went into a financial crisis. Unathi says, "In South Africa, it is countercultural for people to acknowledge that their family has gone from plenty to lack. People don't often complain; they simply adapt and rarely take the time to deal with any pain or trauma." This was not limited to finances.

In 1996 the Truth and Reconciliation Commission was established to provide an opportunity for victims and perpetrators to tell the truth and give and receive apologies. Many perpetrators got amnesty for their crimes. The problem was that not all victims and their families were able to share their stories or find healing, and few perpetrators who were denied amnesty were even tried in court.[12] Although it seemed that many Black South Africans were unaffected, emotional pain, fear, and anger remain below the surface. Unathi has also struggled to work through those feelings and against the internal barrier that caused her to question whether she had the academic ability and the financial resources to succeed in life. Yet she persevered, applied, and was accepted into college in the United States. The first semester ushered in a season of personal and spiritual transformation for her. The Lord revealed to her how her history has affected all aspects of her life.

INTERNALIZED RACISM

Liza's mother and her stepfather were executives at a community organization in Boston's now-designated Latin Quarter. The organization dealt with issues of racism and justice in the community. Her parents worked tirelessly, seven days a week. Liza and her stepsiblings went with their parents to their workplace on weekends. The kids spent their days stuck in a room watching movies and eating TV dinners. Although her parents were involved in justice work, they dealt with chronic stress as they confronted White supremacy and racism. Liza could also see how some community leaders simultaneously internalized racism while actively rejecting racism externally. Preferential treatment seemed to be given to those who had a lighter skin color. When people of color internalize racism, we ingest a poisonous brew that causes us to think and act negatively toward ourselves and others in our communities. We easily collude with personal and systemic racism that reinforces the power and privilege of White people and undermines the authority of people of color.

Liza's mom spoke with a heavy Spanish accent. She was a leader in their community, but outside of it White people would talk slowly to her, as if she were a child, or loudly, as if her hearing was impaired. Some would even speak to Liza instead of her mom because they assumed Liza's mother didn't speak any English. After her mom transitioned from community work and went into banking, she encountered bias from her White colleagues. She faced daily microaggression and had to assert her authority and capacity. Liza's mom had to prove her right to hold leadership positions; triple-checking everything led to her becoming a perfectionist. On more than one occasion while working late, security guards were unresponsive to her requests in the building because they assumed she was a cleaning lady. Liza has taken on the same burden of always having to outperform—being a workaholic—and taking little time for self-care. She battles with being hard on herself and often feels like she's not enough.

Liza walked through life with a suitcase full of unprocessed grief and chronic stress, and she carried these feelings into her marriage and her parenting. She subconsciously decided that the first language of her kids would be English, not Spanish—after all, her husband, Dan, is Korean. Liza did this subconsciously, but one day while in prayer she had an epiphany, the painful truth that although she loves hearing Colombian Spanish, part of her did not want her kids to go through what her mom went through. Liza cried out to the Lord in lament, angry about why she had to deal with the legitimate fear that her kids would be treated poorly or thought of as less than. She uncovered how her self-defeating coping mechanism aimed at keeping her kids from harm had also unintentionally cut them off from their own culture and heritage. Liza no longer wants to pay such a high price for what she can't control. She regrets that they could've learned Spanish earlier. But now they are. Liza now knows that God is for her and her kids. The Lord placed them in a rich culture and heritage that is loved and blessed.

Unathi's class assignments continued to challenge all that she thought was true about being Black and South African. She began to face how she really felt about herself: feeling inferior and fearful and thinking she was in the wrong. Whenever she heard a White person's voice, it triggered anxiety that she was somehow in trouble. Unathi started reading South African history, particularly the history of the Transkei. Apartheid included the economic exploitation of the country's resources and the elimination of cultural pride. Under apartheid the oppressed were made to believe their ways of living and thinking were inferior to the West, and Whiteness was superior.[13] Unathi realized if she understood her history, she'd better understand herself. She learned that in South Africa an inferiority narrative was imposed on Black folks, which was coupled with a fear of White folks. Some Blacks even bought the lie that White is the gold standard such that a Black person who is progressing is called Nnugu (White). Perhaps this is because when some Black folks become prosperous, they often emulate White people in their lifestyle. They become more individualistic and driven, and they speak English rather than their mother tongue. Some rate each other according to their accent; they believe that speaking the Queen's English like a White person helps them to be better perceived. It grieves Unathi to see how she and her community have accepted and played along with the inferiority narrative.

TELLING THE TRUTH

Soong-Chan Rah says, "Lament is honesty before God and each other."[14] People of color often find it hard to trust our hearts to others in matters of loss, grief, and lament, but we absolutely need one another. John Welshons, author of *Awakening from Grief*, writes, "Our job is to be a presence, rather than a savior, a companion, rather than a leader, a friend, rather than a teacher."[15] Instead of

someone merely mouthing words, we need compassionate listeners
who acknowledge: "I see you, and I see your pain." Liza and Unathi
both have friends who understand the importance of tears and
lament rather than only railing in anger or proclaiming that God
has a purpose in pain. These friends mutually process, lament, and
grapple with racism and microaggression and the resulting pain,
anger, trauma, forgiveness, and reconciliation. These kinds of
relationships bring hope in the midst of hurting. We discover that
there are others committed to walking with us on this journey
toward healing and reconciliation.

The first church Liza attended after becoming a Christian was
multiethnic, but the predominant culture was Anglo. The church
started an outreach to the city, and it was troubling to watch the
White leaders or volunteers interact with urban people of color and
churches. Liza realized how they, like herself, often overperson-
alized people's struggles but didn't understand the reality of
systemic oppression. Liza was a member of that church for seven
years, and before moving on she told a pastor, "In my seven years
not one person ever walked up and introduced themselves to me
except those that weren't White." She was the one reaching out and
helping others feel welcome. The pastor gave excuses, and Liza left
the church wondering if it was just her.

When Liza began working with other White Christian leaders,
she saw that racism and bias were alive and well. When attending
their conferences, Liza experienced two things: First, always having
to initiate engagement with White people because they would not
greet her, and, second, often having them look past her to see who
else they could be talking to. At a conference where Liza was a
presenter on a panel that addressed racial reconciliation, a young
African American woman shared how that very day a conference
greeter specifically tasked with greeting people as they walked into
the plenary session greeted the two White people who walked in

ahead of her but didn't greet her, as if she were invisible. The experience was painful. There will always be a remnant who speak the Lord's truth even if nothing changes. Liza hopes to remain true to what she believes: the fact that Jesus is still Jesus. He overcomes systemic oppression and heals individuals and communities, and she can join him in that work.

Soong-Chan Rah notes, "The church should become the place where the fullness of suffering is expressed in a safe environment. Liturgy, worship, leadership, small groups and other aspects of church life should provide the safe place where the fullness of suffering can be set free."[16] Unathi's church offered such a safe space for her to heal. The congregation went through a teaching series on race and racism. This was the first time that Unathi openly expressed her heart and hurt in front of White people. Because of her transparency, members of the church connect group she was a part of also opened up. On Sundays she could go to church and allow her feelings to surface, and there was no rush to get over it. Something powerful happened the day she shared her story in front of White people and asked them, "How are you not racist?" As she prayed by herself and with others and allowed the pain to move through her, healing came. In the midst of this season her dad passed away, and this pushed her even deeper into spaces where she has more love and compassionate toward others. The blinders of racial trauma are now removed, so she can see opportunities to take rather than self-selecting out. As she releases her grief, her confidence has risen. She no longer believes she shouldn't speak up, must stay at the back, and should never challenge authority.

When King David hears of Rizpah's tenacity in guarding her loved ones, he finally grants her justice. He commands his soldiers to gather the bones of Rizpah's sons along with the bones of King Saul and his son Jonathan and bury them in their family tomb at Zelah. After King David relents and treats Rizpah's sons with dignity, the blessing of the Lord is released on the land (2 Samuel 21).

I wonder to what degree the church's refusal to recognize the grief and pain of people of color and refusal to lament has affected our land.

ACTIVISM

Activism is often a byproduct of lament. Although our grief diminishes, it may never fully leave. However, as we grow we may discover that it leads to something new. Activism is often a by-product of grief and lament. Isaiah 1:17 says,

> Learn to do good;
> seek justice,
>   rescue the oppressed,
> defend the orphan,
>   plead for the widow.

Unathi and Liza are learning how Christ-centered activism can contribute toward personal and collective healing. The speeches and writings of Martin Luther King Jr. inspire Liza while Nelson Mandela's autobiography, *Long Walk to Freedom*, inspires Unathi. When under great trial and duress these men cried out in lament for mercy and justice for their people. Much like Rizpah, they refused to be ignored; they persevered.

Unathi and Liza are prayer warriors who lament the trauma and suffering of others and intercede for them in prayer. Recently, Liza prioritized lament as an essential spiritual practice and made it the focus of the yearly day of prayer for the Christian organization she helps lead. This meant explicitly addressing systemic racism within and outside of the organization. The staff spent the day in small groups praying and sharing stories of lament in regard to what is happening in society and to them personally. It was the most profound prayer day Liza has participated in because people shared honestly about their deep, personal emotional pain, anger, and fear. They also expressed pain related to the work they do as they confront systemic oppression. They weren't hiding their vulnerability or trying to keep their distance. Liza's team needed an emotionally healthy space, and they found one that day.

Liza is vigilant on behalf of the people of color around her. While driving, she is aware of cars being pulled over and looks to see if it's a Brown or Black person. She slows down and makes eye contact with the driver. Liza will give a thumbs up, thumbs down to see if everything's all right. That's the level of awareness she believes she has to have. It is exhausting, but the alternative is denial or inattentiveness that could cost a life. Liza is an activist who is teaching her kids the skills needed to fight any instinct they may have to marginalize others. Her kids are also learning to be like their courageous mom and pray, speak up, and act when they see someone being marginalized.

Liza and Unathi's healing journeys have shown us that as we cry out to God in prayers of lament over past and current injustices, he meets us in our pain. We see the need to work through the hardest part, forgiving our oppressors. Knowing that we will confront racism again, Jesus says we are to leave the punishment of our oppressors to him, and we are to forgive: "Not seven times, but, I tell you, seventy-seven times" (Matthew 18:22).

If we harbor any internalized racism, it must be renounced and repented of so we can fully accept our identity and heritage. We can release ourselves from judgment and forgive ourselves just as God has. Isaiah 61:3 reminds us that the Holy Spirit is present

to provide for those who mourn in Zion—
  to give them a garland instead of ashes,

the oil of gladness instead of mourning,
the mantle of praise instead of a faint spirit.
They will be called oaks of righteousness,
the planting of the LORD, to display his glory.

We are like mighty oaks; from humble beginnings we've slowly grown, and with faith and endurance, we are strong and resilient. Isaiah 61 goes on to say,

They shall build up the ancient ruins,
they shall raise up the former devastations;
they shall repair the ruined cities,
the devastations of many generations. (v. 4)

As we provide safe and sacred spaces for lament, comfort, and healing, we become impregnable and discover that we already have the resources we need to restore our communities.

REFLECTION AND PRAYER PROMPTS

1. Can you be honest with God and share your full range of feelings with him? If not, why?

2. Write out a prayer of lament to God.

3. In prayer, ask for the Lord's comfort through Scripture, words, or images that assure you of his presence.

CHAPTER SEVEN

SHAME

You wore your identity as a
Coat one size too small,
Irritating from the constricting
Fit of history.
Neither America nor Africa
Could break your self-hate,
As if the ebony clay
You were molded in
was a fruit too bitter
To consume.

JONATHAN ROWE, "PARADIGM OF REJECTION"

A few years before I married Nick, he was pursuing a PhD while living in Boston's Hyde Square, a mostly Dominican, Puerto Rican, and African American inner-city community. He had a desire to make a difference in the community, so he volunteered with Young Life as an outreach worker to at-risk youth of color. The Young Life center was based in a three-story (triple decker) house where Nick, the White program director, and a team of mostly Black men offered mentoring, tutoring, academic advising, and recreation at no cost. On the night of October 23, 1989, an incident stunned Nick, the community, and the country. Charles Stuart, a White man, called 911 to report that minutes after leaving a birthing class at Brigham and Women's Hospital in Mission Hill, a six-foot tall Black man with a raspy voice wearing a black sweatsuit shot him in the stomach and his wife Carol in the head. The city and the nation believed Charles, and the Boston police invaded the Mission Hill community. They rode into area housing developments in patrol cars and on horseback looking for the shooter. Black males were rounded up as suspects and then openly humiliated by frisks and strip searches. Onlookers assumed the men to be criminals.

A few nights later, after a long youth meeting, Nick offered to drive some of the teens to their apartment in Mission Hill. When the teens ran from Nick's car, they were stopped, frisked, and roughed up by roving police officers. Nick sat quietly in his Honda Civic praying that the situation would not escalate and that he would go unnoticed.

The next day the teens arrived at the Young Life center racially traumatized, their hurt and anger overflowing with tears and threats of retaliation. But they were defenseless without anyone to advocate on their behalf. The city and the nation got swept up into the Stuart narrative. A Black man was arrested and assumed to be the killer. Later on, Charles's brother Matthew confessed that the Black man held in custody was not guilty—his brother, Charles, had killed Carol and shot himself. On January 3, 1990, as the full story became known, Charles Stuart took his lies with him as he jumped off Boston's Tobin Bridge to his death. The *Los Angeles Times* reported, "Was Stuart's suspected plot to kill his wife so extra-ordinarily cunning that an entire city cannot be faulted for having been duped? Or did Boston also fall victim to its own prejudices and stereotypes when it ignored inconsistencies in

Stuart's story and launched a manhunt that tore apart a racially mixed neighborhood?"[1]

Although Nick and the team had a lot to say about the deception in the Stuart case, they never fully processed the emotional injury inflicted on the teens. The city of Boston made excuses for their response but never offered an official apology to the Black males in the community. The only thing Nick knew to do was to deny the racial trauma, wear a mask of indifference to hide his shame that he was helpless, and keep it moving. Nick learned this way of navigating through life from his parents.

PAMELA AND WINSTON

Nick's mom, Pamela, was born in Port-of-Spain, Trinidad, and moved to the United Kingdom for nursing school when she was eighteen years old. She lived under the guardianship of her uncle George, an immigrant from Trinidad, and Aunt Rose, his White wife from London. Pam was the queen of the *code-switch*, a term that reflects how effortlessly her accent changed from West Indian patois to the Queen's English, depending on the company she kept. This helped her to persevere through nursing training while living in North London during the 1950s. Pam became an exceptional midwifery nurse, a statuesque woman with a heart and nurturing presence so vast that even the most colicky babies would nestle in her bosom and quickly be lulled to sleep. At the age of thirty, Pam married Winston, an immigrant to the United Kingdom from St. Elizabeth Parish, Jamaica, and ten years her senior. Winston was an aspiring engineer.

Soon Winston and Pam were parents to three kids, Nicholas and his twin sisters. Winston carried on with his studies, but he faced systemic racism and classism in the UK educational system. His college professors had low expectations of him and often ignored or belittled him. Even as he was prevented from advancing, he began assisting White master's degree students in their projects. Each night Winston came home sullen and with a short fuse. Conversation with his family was limited, and playtimes with his kids were infrequent; interactions were mostly for disciplinary reasons if at all. Each morning Winston left for work wearing an unseen mask of shame to hide his deep disappointment.

THE IMPOSTOR

An immigrant's story can seem heroic, but sometimes it includes shame, silent pain, and a mask. Shame is not the same as guilt, an emotion that arises when we have in fact done something wrong. People of color may carry shame accompanied by internalized racism that says it is not what you've done but who you are that's wrong. Because of shame, we feel we are defective, unacceptable, incompetent, or fundamentally damaged goods. Shame tells us who and what we aren't, but God tells us who and what we are and what we can do.

Although Brené Brown's research doesn't specifically address the roots and impact of shame on people of color, she does bring to light some important truths: "Shame keeps us from telling our own stories and prevents us from listening to others tell their stories. . . . We silence our voices and keep our secrets out of the fear of disconnection."[2]

Too often, rather than being ourselves, people of color present a false image that affects how we view ourselves and how we relate to others. We have lives full of "should" and "ought to," and when confronted with any personal limitations, we experience deep shame. When we wear a mask rather than deal with reality, we can become overly responsible and end up carrying burdens that we were not meant to bear. We live a double life. There is a big difference between how we are at home and who we are in public, or who we are on the inside and on the outside.

According to the American Psychological Association, impostor syndrome is a significant struggle for women and people of color.[3] Impostor syndrome is not about the low self-esteem of people of color. Experiences of racism cause people of color to feel powerless. Although we are still able to function, the sting remains. A consequence of racism is that it becomes internalized by people of color across socioeconomic lines. This causes some folks to struggle to accept their God-given abilities and accomplishments. Others have been repeatedly told that they are inadequate or less than, and soon they believe it. People of color can't be open about their feelings, needs, or struggles with worthiness when they are in an environment where they are labeled an impostor. This was Winston and Pam's story.

There are biblical stories of people who wear the mask of false bravado while struggling to admit their brokenness and need; others struggle with their greatness. In John 4 Jesus goes out of his way to have a divine appointment with a Samaritan woman at a well. Although everyone else came to the well in the earlier and cooler part of the day, this woman chose to come in the heat of the day when she would not be seen. She wanted to avoid the glances and the whispers. She wore a figurative mask to isolate herself from others. We do the same, and we too know the loneliness of not having anyone meet us in our pain. But Jesus met her just like he meets us; he comes where and when we least expect him. The encounter is remarkable because as a Jew, Jesus should not be speaking to her. She was a mixed-race Samaritan woman, whose status was considered just above that of cattle and who was thought to be unclean. Like most of us, she had a past full of things done to her and choices made by her that contributed to who she became. Like many of us, she had experiences that gave her negative messages about herself, her race, and God.

TRANSITIONS

As the years rolled by without a college degree, Winston and Pam realized that the options for Winston were limited, given the social restrictions of class and race in the United Kingdom. Sometimes the Lord opens an unexpected door. When Nick was eleven and his sisters were eight, the family immigrated to the United States, carrying only their most precious belongings in suitcases. Other doors opened when Winston found employment at the New York Institute of Technology as a supervisor of an engineering lab and completed his degree, confirming for him that the roadblocks he faced in the United Kingdom were race-based. Although Winston and Pam were self-sufficient, the strain of building a new life drove them to a small Assembly of God church where they recommitted their lives to Christ. Almost overnight Winston became more relaxed after work, and weekends were opportunities for fun. Sundays, in particular, were now focused on the Lord and family. Nick felt he'd finally gotten the father he always wanted.

For Pam, the transition was not as rosy. She carried considerable responsibility and authority as a midwifery nurse in the United Kingdom. In the United States midwifery was not as well respected. And Pam was a Black woman who refused to "stay in her place." Arguments were frequent with doctors who used forceps and other invasive techniques, or relied heavily and unnecessarily on cesarean sections to remove babies from the womb. Pam could no longer be part of a system that violated her deeply held personal values. She became a conventional nurse, and it was not long before her nursing skills would come in handy when Winston experienced frequent and painful urination. His doctor brushed them off repeatedly after checkups and general tests revealed nothing.

Research studies have shown that because of systemic racism there is significant bias in the quality of medical treatment received according to one's racial group. Black men are more likely to experience treatment delays and postoperative complications dealing with cancer of the prostate than White men.[4] Because of Pam's insistence, Winston finally got a second opinion. The new doctor returned with a troubling diagnosis of moderately advanced prostate cancer. Pam helped Winston navigate the medical establishment to get proper treatment, and he eventually went into remission.

THE CATECHISM

Pam and Winston believed that education was the ticket to success in the world. On Nick's first day of school, Pam sat him down and recited an instruction that he and his sisters after him would call "The Catechism"—betraying their Anglican roots. She told Nick that he is a Black boy in a White world, and White people will expect him to do poorly or they'd have no expectations of him at all. Each week she'd remind him that he was gifted but could not be just as good as his White classmates; he had to blow away the competition. A long-standing consequence was that Nick often felt like an impostor. W. E. B. Du Bois wrote, "It is a peculiar sensation, this double-consciousness, this sense of always looking at one's self through the eyes of others, of measuring one's soul by the tape of a world that looks on in amused contempt and pity."[5] Nick accepted the lie of shame and self-hatred that said there must be something defective about him because he had to do extra things to get noticed. Somehow, just being himself was not good enough. His anger was directed outwards in two directions: anger toward White people who set up standards of acceptance and benefited from systemic racism, and anger directed toward other Blacks who were not meeting that standard or who messed up his game.

Nick worked hard and it paid off. Pam and Winston proudly announced to their church family that Nick was accepted into

Massachusetts Institution of Technology (MIT). The summer before his freshman year Nick received an invitation to participate in an academic and student support program for incoming students of color. Nick didn't participate, partly because he thought he didn't need it, and partly because he feared being labeled as a person of color who got into MIT because they lowered their standards. During his first semester Nick began experiencing stereotype threats, and by the end of the term his fear was realized as his grades were flailing. Nick was fundamentally lonely. He trusted no one, neither Whites nor Blacks. He created an emotional wall around himself that cut him off from authentic relationships. He wore a mask and retreated into the books and excelling at school. In doing so, Nick ran away from his pain and anger over the situation. Because he didn't want to be hurt, he morphed and assimilated. His White friends would say of him, "When I think about you, I don't think that you are Black." This was not good news, because Nick is Black and comes with a culture and a legacy. Nick disavowed this when he wore the mask, and White people disavowed it when they didn't see him in his totality.

During Nick's freshman year his dad's cancer returned with a vengeance, and by his sophomore year his father passed away. That year, while trying to deal with such great loss, Nick was belittled by a racist professor who took every opportunity to engage in microaggressions to communicate to Nick that he did not belong. Nick watched his professor fully engage with White students, but the professor either ignored him or was straight faced with hints of contempt. Nick didn't know how to respond and feared the consequence if he did.

In some cases when we have issues with authority figures, we either react in open rebellion against them, or because we feel it's too risky, we do not speak the truth nor do we trust ourselves or others. Instead, we become passive-aggressive or manipulative in an attempt to get our message across. People of color may respond this way because of the fear of retaliation. It is difficult to say what we really feel, so the result is a lot of confusion. We may not know what we want because we have never had the chance to express our hearts. When we feel diminished or shamed, we may lash out in anger as a form of retaliation.

Nick did not process the grief over the loss of his father. It was impossible for him to see how the impostor syndrome was affecting him while he was in a place where he was told that he was an impostor. Nick passed the course and later graduated from MIT. He still wore a mask and thought, *Maybe Mom's catechism was right.*

PHILADELPHIA

It took another five years before Nick had a pivotal experience that helped him to heal from racial trauma and find freedom from the impostor syndrome. He participated in an emotional healing conference in Philadelphia that literally transformed his life. When Nick arrived at the healing conference he had little hope for change. Yet he prayed for insight and healing, particularly about why it was difficult to emotionally connect with Jonathan, our then two-year-old son. As the conference drew to a close, Nick sat alone, an emotionless impostor. During the closing prayer, I asked a Black man to pray with Nick. As the man prayed, grief washed over Nick. He doubled over, wailing loudly and was thoroughly broken as he began to see how interpersonal and generational racial trauma caused him to close off emotionally from his son. He was repeating his mom's attempt to prepare her Black son for the harsh realities of life—and he was as disconnected from his Black son as his father had been. Another man came and prayed, and a grave disappointment surfaced as Nick spoke of how he finally got the father he always wanted only to have him snatched away. All those years he felt he wasn't allowed to feel his disappointment. His cries were deep and guttural as he finally tapped into the well of pain he carried when his dad passed away during the fall of his sophomore year.

A NEW SOURCE

Beyond our hiding or the robust and defiant face that we put on, Jesus knows where we've been and who we really are. In John 4:13-16 the woman at the well wants water, but what she really needs is water that will quench her deepest thirst. Jesus responds to the woman, "Everyone who drinks of this water will be thirsty again, but those who drink of the water that I will give them will never be thirsty. The water that I will give will become in them a spring of water gushing up to eternal life." The Holy Spirit brings us into all truth, which includes the fact that behind the mask is a person in need of a Savior. When we come to the Lord just as we are—vulnerable, fearful, and needy—he meets us there and confronts the lies we believe about him, ourselves, and others. He exchanges the lies for the truth that we are loved, forgiven, and transformed. He heals the deep well of shame within us.

After her encounter with Jesus, the woman left her water jar, a subtle but meaningful metaphor. Jesus is now her new source and means of getting her deepest needs met. The woman promptly went into town to spread the good news that the Christ had come. She said to the men, "Come and see a Man Who told me everything I ever did! Can this be the Christ?" The people later said to the woman, "Now we believe! It is no longer because of what you said about Jesus, but we have heard Him ourselves. We know, for sure, that He is the Christ, the One Who saves men of this world from the punishment of their sins" (John 4:29, 42 NLV).

Just like the woman at the well, Nick no longer needed to wear a mask and isolate himself from his family and community. His heart had been like the rose of Jericho or the resurrection plant.

During the dry season the small gray branches of the plant curl up forming a ball that covers its seedpods. It is one of a few plants known for their ability to survive desiccation. The plant can actually survive this way for years. It looks like it's dead; however, when it receives water, its leaves quickly turn green, and it produces tiny white flowers. With every teardrop, Nick became more alive and resilient. He knows that he will face shaming and racism in the future, so he is diligent about the choices he makes in his thoughts and actions. He continues to need others he can process things with and pray about any future racist incidents and significant racial trauma.

For the past twenty-five years, Nick has met monthly with a supportive group of Black, White, and Brown Christian men: Bil, Scott, and Bill. They call themselves MMOG (mighty men of God); they openly share their struggles and triumphs and pray for one another. These brothers in Christ help Nick see his blind spots: when he is falling into perfectionism or comparison. When Nick is feeling overwhelmed because of racism and life in general and is tempted to hide behind a mask or believe the impostor syndrome's lies, the men speak truth to him. They challenge him to ask for help or, at other times, not to take himself so seriously. They tell Nick that he is not alone and his life matters. They remind Nick of what Jesus says about him in the Word and that he is unconditionally loved by God and them.

In Isaiah 61:7 we read,

> Because their shame was double,
>   and dishonor was proclaimed as their lot,
> therefore they shall possess a double portion;
>   everlasting joy shall be theirs.

After the woman met Jesus at the well, she was freed from shame and received a double portion of blessing in her land. The Lord does the same for each of us. He sees in us something more profound than what the world would tell us. He sees people of color lovingly created to bear his image and likeness and be redeemed by his grace. Jesus says that who we truly are is found in and through him. As we lay down our masks and shame and surrender our pain to Jesus (just as Nick did), we begin to see that the Lord has already bestowed honor on us. We discover the many ways that he blesses us right where we are, as people of color beloved of the Lord. No longer in hiding, we are empowered by the Holy Spirit to free others from the weight of shame.

REFLECTION AND PRAYER PROMPTS

1. Ask the Lord to reveal the source of any hidden shame you feel.

2. Are you ready to lay down your shame? If so, how would this change you, your life, or that of others?

3. Ask the Lord to identify if there are people who shame you and also how you diminish and shame yourself for not "measuring up."

CHAPTER EIGHT

ADDICTION

*Before you can
break out of prison
you must realize
you are locked up.*

Anonymous

Interracial marriage was illegal in Virginia under the 1924 Act to Preserve Racial Integrity. This antimiscegenation law stipulated that anyone with a drop of nonwhite or mixed-race ancestry would be considered "Colored" and subject to the laws that upheld racial segregation and criminalized marriage between White and Colored folks. The law was still on the books in 1958 when longtime friends Richard Loving, a White man, and Mildred Jeter, a woman of African American and First Nation ancestry, fell in love and got engaged.

Since it was unlawful for them to marry in their hometown of Central Point in Caroline County, Virginia, they traveled to Washington, DC, where interracial marriage was legal. They were married in July 1958 and returned home to Virginia, where they risked felony charges and imprisonment of one to five years in

Virginia's state prison. On July 11, 1958, at 2 a.m., the local sheriff burst into the Lovings' bedroom, and as he shined his flashlight on the couple, he shouted, "What are you doing in bed with this woman?" Mildred responded, "I'm his wife." The couple's plea for mercy was denied, and they were arrested on charges of violating Virginia's antimiscegenation law.[1] At the trial, Richard and Mildred pleaded guilty, and Judge Leon M. Bazile sentenced them to one year in prison but agreed to suspend the sentence if the couple left Virginia, never to return for twenty-five years. The couple agreed, left their home and extended family in Virginia, and moved to Washington, DC. Over the next five years they had three kids but longed to return to Virginia. In 1963 the American Civil Liberties Union took up their case and filed a motion to have their conviction and sentences overturned. The *Loving v. Virginia* Supreme Court case went before the US Supreme Court in April 1967. The Lovings' attorney passionately proclaimed that the antimiscegenation laws "are not health and welfare laws. These are slavery laws, pure and simple."[2] On June 12, 1967, almost nine years after Richard and Mildred got married, the Supreme Court in a unanimous decision found that Virginia's interracial marriage law violated the Fourteenth Amendment to the Constitution. The justices overturned the 1958 criminal conviction of Richard and Mildred Loving and also the laws against interracial marriage in Virginia and fifteen other states across the country.

ED AND CAROL

In 1955, three years before the Lovings were married, Ed, an African American man, and Carol, a White woman, met at church and struck up a friendship. In addition to their racial difference, these two were raised in vastly different worlds. Carol grew up in the North in a beige colonial house in a White middle-class suburb. Her mom was a homemaker, and her dad was a scientist. Ed was from the Midwest, where his single mom worked as a house maid.

His family lived on the outskirts of town in a one-room shack. Ed and Carol fell in love despite their pastor pronouncing from the pulpit that interracial dating and marriage were unwise and unbiblical. As they carefully read the Scriptures, they could not find a theological basis for racial segregation, so they got engaged. When Carol's family heard about the engagement, they threatened to disown her if she went through with the marriage. Carol and Ed prayed and decided to go forward with their marriage but did not ask their pastor to officiate the wedding, knowing he'd refuse. Somehow the word went out to other local churches, and pastors were threatened with dismissal if they performed the marriage ceremony. Ed was in seminary at the time, and as he shared his struggle, the chaplain agreed to marry the couple. In fall 1956, Carol and Ed were married. A few friends were supportive, but other friends told them that their union would damage their future kids.

A *Psychology Today* report noted that "mixed-race individuals can also be targeted by a unique kind of prejudice that is rarely discussed these days: anti-miscegenation. A current manifestation of this belief can be seen by those who advocate for the preservation of authenticity or racial purity because traditions will be lost through cultural dilution or racial mixing."[3] This may be one of the excuses used by Carol's family for why they strongly disapproved of the marriage. However, when Carol became pregnant and gave birth to a son, Tom, the rift with her parents started to mend. Several years later, the family moved into a bigger house in a White neighborhood where they were the only biracial family. Tom remembers that during his first week the neighborhood kids were hanging out on a front porch innocently playing when a chorus of unwelcoming words were shouted as he passed: "Nigger, we don't want you here." The words cut deeply into Tom's heart. Over time a few of the kids became his friends, but being a mixed-race person was confusing to Tom. Research has shown that "although some children choose to adopt one ethnic affiliation, forcing children to categorize themselves with one category and therefore denying their multiplicity is associated with greater anxiety and lower self-esteem."[4] Tom entered young adulthood bearing the anxiety of racial-identity confusion and a perfectionist streak, all of which contributed to his developing an addiction.

ADDICTION

No one decides to be an addict. Addiction is a glorified pain reliever. We engage in addictive behaviors for a reason. When the pain of racial trauma becomes so great, we want to numb ourselves, so we use addictive behavior to help us function and carry on with our lives. Addictions come in all shapes and sizes. We try to numb our pain through many means: alcohol, drugs, pornography, or gambling. Legitimate activities are also addictive: compulsive TV watching, the internet (not just pornography), work, bad relationships (whether sexual or not), food, and drugs prescribed for legitimate reasons. Addiction occurs after repeated, compulsive use of a substance or thing despite the negative consequences.

Psychologically, the process is called *conditioning*, and the spiritual term is called *attachment*. Attachment links our passion to someone or something that promises to give us relief. This attachment produces addiction, and once it takes hold we are bound to that person, place, substance, behavior, or belief. Over time, we need more and more of the "pain reliever" to obtain the same effect. When we numb ourselves, we do not address the root cause—we only put a bandage over a bleeding, gaping wound in hope that it will heal. And it never does. Addiction is a created distraction, a distortion of reality, and a common phase in twelve-step groups: "All addictions are cunning, baffling, powerful and insidious."[5] The insanity of acting out of our addiction is that we seek relief from the very thing that causes it. That addiction is the "golden calf" that we read about in Exodus 32—it holds out the promise of relief, but in fact it is empty and can't deliver.

The golden calf. In the book of Exodus, the story of the golden calf may not seem to be a story about addiction, but as we take a close look at it, we can see the connection. The Israelites were camped at the base of Mount Sinai waiting for their leader, Moses, to return from the summit, where he went to receive instructions from God. The Israelites became uneasy because Moses was gone a very long time. They were in the middle of the wilderness and were vulnerable to the changing weather, wild animals, and potentially hostile armies.

It's understandable why they were anxious. Since they had spent their entire lives in slavery they didn't know how to defend themselves. They became more anxious and agitated and said to Aaron, Moses' brother, "Come, make gods for us, who shall go before us" (v. 1). This calf was probably a symbol of a familiar Egyptian deity. Aaron gave in and answered, "Take off the gold rings that are on the ears of your wives, your sons, and your daughters, and bring them to me" (v. 2). Aaron "took the gold from them, formed it in a mold, and cast an image of a calf; and they said, 'These are your gods, O Israel, who brought you up out of the land of Egypt!'" (v. 4). An altar was built for the golden calf, and the Israelites worshiped and offered sacrifices to it, and the next day they partied. The story of the golden calf serves as a model of idolatry and addiction.

It took years before Tom saw that his addiction was an idol and that he engaged it in the same way the Israelites engaged the golden calf. The roots that later sprung forth in addiction were created early in Tom's life. He grew up feeling as if people were always watching and waiting for him to make a wrong move. He sensed from an early age that it was his responsibility to vindicate his parents for their rebellious act of miscegenation. At the same time, Tom found it difficult to find a solid sense of his racial identity.

For many multiracial kids, their "parents' apprehensions over cultural dilution may lead to their insistence on raising their children in a mono-racial framework."[6] This was not the case with Tom; his White mother made sure that Tom learned about his African American heritage, and his Black dad was in many ways Eurocentric in his taste and lifestyle. Because of this Tom felt isolated. He knew he was not White but wondered if he was "Black enough." At the same time, he believed that he also had to represent all Black people. Saera Kahn writes that "mixed race individuals often report feeling alienated from their own cultural groups because they are deemed not 'authentic enough' or appear too racially ambiguous to be accepted. They report that their yearning for acceptance and community from these groups pressures them to choose 'sides' and conform to one of their monoracial categories."[7]

Tom experienced pressure from always having to be "on," which meant that he could not rest in a place of acceptance. Because there was no place for Tom to let down his guard, he could never be himself. Tom chose a habit that was quiet and closeted. Pornography provided the way of escape for Tom to find relief from these debilitating feelings on his terms. Whatever form our addiction takes, it is an idol that we create, worship, and sacrifice to, and we need to demolish it.

Worship. When Tom got to college, his internal good boy persona started to shatter, and he increasingly became involved in pornography. Tom says, "The bottom line is I secretly worshiped women's bodies. I hate to say that, but I was convinced that my salvation lay there, even while I was walking with the Lord and knew the Word inside and out." Tom somehow found a place within himself to allow for a double life that nobody knew.

While at college Tom met Donna, and they became close friends. After graduation, their relationship turned romantic. Unfortunately, Donna had only a vague idea of the intensity of Tom's secret struggle. By the time they married, Tom was a full-blown porn addict.

Sacrifice. As the years went on, Tom's acting-out behavior escalated. What used to be "unthinkable" now became "must do." He crossed boundary line after boundary line, and his double life became more and more refined. People looked at him as a good husband, father, minister, and disciple, with a great command of the Word. But no one knew he was also an out-of-control addict. In his journal, just before his secret life was exposed, he wrote, "The most devastating consequence of this is that it ruins my relationship with God." One night Tom was out doing something he had no business doing. He felt hopeless because he tried to fix himself and failed. He screamed at the top of his lungs, "I don't love you, God. I don't believe you can help me. You've abandoned me!" Tom lived there for a while. He sacrificed his relationship with the Lord, because at that point he had no evidence that healing was possible. He was on the verge of sacrificing other things as well: marriage, career, and family—even his life. This would have been a huge price to pay for addictive behaviors that now gave him less and less satisfaction.

Demolish. When Moses came down from the mountain and saw the golden calf, he was furious. Maybe he knew that as long as the idol stood on the altar, it would lure the Israelites. The calf would anesthetize them so they could avoid addressing their fears. Moses burned the calf in a fire, ground it to powder, scattered it on the water, and made the Israelites drink it. Perhaps by his action Moses wanted to drive home the point that their idol was powerless and incapable of quenching their thirst, giving peace, or satisfying their longings. The journey of healing and transformation required Tom to surrender his self-sufficiency to the Lord and receive help to stop, look, listen, and walk forward.

Stop and look. Like the Israelites' golden calf, Tom's addiction needed to be demolished. But first he had to come out of denial and see how his addictive behaviors had only made his life miserable. He decided that whatever it took, he had to stop. He had to stop numbing the pain of racial trauma with the anesthesia of addiction and instead submit to the painful and invasive surgery of God's healing work. Tom recognized that Jesus is not only a skillful surgeon but has gone through the same battle. Jesus knows how we feel. He understands. He feels our pain. Hebrews 4:15 says, "We do not have a high priest who is unable to sympathize with our weaknesses, but we have one who in every respect has been tested as we are, yet without sin."

Desperate to find peace and healing, Tom started attending a twelve-step program and began the journey toward dismantling his addiction. In the twelve-step program Tom had to honestly answer some tough questions. The answers were disturbing, and the fact that he had to tell his sponsor and accountability partners was humbling. Tom admitted that though he said, "That's the last time I will do that," he fell over and over again. He had to admit that to get the same relief he had to go deeper into the behavior and increasingly found himself doing things he'd never imagined he would do. Most importantly, Tom had to admit that the addiction had power over him. Though he tried, he couldn't stop. In his letter to the Romans, Paul describes the situation perfectly:

> So I find this law at work: Although I want to do good, evil is right there with me. For in my inner being I delight in God's law; but I see another law at work in me, waging war against the law of my mind and making me a prisoner of the law of sin at work within me. What a wretched man I am! Who will rescue me from this body that is subject to death?

Thanks be to God, who delivers me through Jesus Christ our Lord. (Romans 7:21-25 NIV)

In his twelve-step group, Tom went through the process of unearthing every behavior and context in which he acted out. He wrote it down and read it to his sponsor. When he did that, he had reliable evidence that his addiction had ruined him. Tom had to look at this squarely and objectively. Tom saw how he became a liar and deceitful; he even deceived himself by denying, respinning, or minimizing the extent of his acting out. On the few days that he had victory and did not fall, he was left so strung out that he was an easy target the next day. This was not victory; it was a delay.

Tom's transformation was a process—over time things changed. With the disciplines of the twelve-step group; the support of family, church, and friends; putting in place practical boundaries to minimize temptation; therapy; and most of all God's grace; the vice grip of sexual addiction loosened. Tom moved into a lifestyle of freedom, transparency, and integrity. He has since become active in the recovery movement and mentors others who are struggling with porn and other addictions. But there was more work to be done in his heart.

Listen and walk. Our pain comes from somewhere, and Jesus wants to deal with more than just the symptoms. We have to listen to the Lord and examine our lives for the causes: Why the pain in the first place? What wound is there that needs healing? True healing must address the root causes of the wounds we try to avoid in the first place. Tom had to pray and listen for what set him up for addiction. Like the Israelites, there was a point in Tom's life when he feared that God had left him and he was on his own. He found that the Holy Spirit could reveal and heal the source of that lie.

A Pew Research survey in 2015 found that many multiracial adults, like other racial minorities, have experienced some type of racial discrimination—racist slurs, poor service in restaurants or other businesses, being unfairly stopped by the police, physical threats—because of their racial background.[8] Those experiences are compounded when "fears of rejection and marginalization from their home ethnic groups has also culminated into greater unhealthy and risk-taking behaviors compared to their mono-racial peers."[9]

Tom had many racially traumatizing experiences. There have been moments in Tom's life when he had to choose to stay at the foot of Mount Sinai and wait rather than to grab for an idol or pain reliever. Psalm 69:32-33 served as a reminder:

> Let the oppressed see it and be glad;
>   you who seek God, let your hearts revive.
> For the LORD hears the needy,
>   and does not despise his own that are in bonds.

Tom says, "It took years of waiting before some truths finally traveled from my head to my heart." The first time it happened Tom was talking with a friend who shared about her journey of acceptance after her daughter married a Black man. Now she has biracial grandkids. For her own sake and for the sake of her grandkids, she had to confront her own racism. So did extended family members. As she spoke, something broke open in Tom. He realized that the former pastor of his parents' church (and the whole church by their silence) had cursed him and his parents. They said that his parents' marriage was doomed, and by implication their biracial child should not exist. Tom saw the spiritual and natural consequences for him, but more importantly he actually felt the wound in his heart. He had lived insecure and unsure of his right to exist. During the prayer time with his friend, Tom had a powerful experience of renouncing those lies and saw them being uprooted from his heart. He was reminded that the Lord created him and loves him just as he is, a biracial man.

BRIDGE BUILDING

Eventually, Tom returned to his parents' former church and shared his story with one of the current pastors. Even though this pastor wasn't born at the time of the events Tom described, on behalf of the church, he offered a heartfelt apology. Tom accepted this apology, but for Tom this was more than just about hearing the pastor say, "please, forgive us." It was about returning to the place where he was cursed, confronting racial trauma, and releasing any unforgiveness he still held. Tom laughs at how the Lord sometimes brings justice in the strangest ways. When he interviewed for his current position, a portrait of the former pastor, long deceased, hung on the wall. The interview went well, and Tom looked at the portrait, smiled, and thought to himself, *How do you like me now?* As Tom walks into the future, he is being filled with the Holy Spirit and thus can serve better and make better choices. His identity is no longer an out-of-control pornography junkie, nor is it one of racial confusion and isolation. Tom is a biracial man who is becoming more and more like Jesus.

When we ultimately surrender our way of being and doing to God and submit to his loving hand, our victory rests on our relationship with him. Jesus meets us in our pain, and the work of Jesus on the cross heals the racial trauma that has empowered our addictions and brings peace through the Holy Spirit. Prayer and accountability from others are also critical because recovering addicts are notorious for lying to ourselves and making excuses for our behavior. Like Tom, it is not enough to clean out the junk; we must fill our lives with something holy and right, and only God can help us to prioritize that. As we keep moving forward, we might get a sense of one of the eternal purposes we were created for.

Tom believes that bridge building has always been part of his calling as a biracial person, but now in this fractured world it's more urgent. Even as we are healing from racial trauma and addiction, we can join Tom in bridging the racial divide.

REFLECTION AND PRAYER PROMPTS

1. List specific behaviors or activities that are now off-limits to you.

2. Identify your triggers. I know that I am most likely in a cycle when the following happens:

3. Write out the thoughts you think to convince yourself that acting out is all right.

4. What truths do you know that can counter these thoughts?

5. What specific actions can you take when you become aware that you are being triggered, preoccupied with addictive thoughts and issues, or tempted?

CHAPTER NINE

FREEDOM

History, despite its wrenching pain,
Cannot be unlived, but if faced
With courage, need not be lived again.

MAYA ANGELOU, *ON THE PULSE OF MORNING*

In South Africa my husband Nick was assigned to a small group with five English- and Afrikaans-speaking White South African men. The irony could not have been more obvious. Inside, Nick was having a fierce debate with God: *Hey! These are not the people I would have chosen for my healing!* To which the Holy Spirit replied, *I am with you. I know what I am doing. And it is this way or no way.* As the Lord began to surface the emotions that Nick had denied, he began to feel the depth of his emotional burden and pain. Gently but firmly the Lord impressed on him that now was the time to remove his mask and become vulnerable with the men in his small group. These men represented the oppressors to Nick. He felt like it was a huge request for him to disclose his brokenness and imperfection to those men. He wrestled with this for twenty-four hours before he returned to the group. He took his seat in the group circle and shared the story of the racism and racial trauma he and his parents had experienced.

The small group members began to pray for Nick, and he heard the Holy Spirit say, *Now it's time to let it go.* Suddenly Nick hunched over, and twenty-five years of pain, anger, and rage came out at once. In the midst of the grief and pain, Nick's moral injury was exposed when he asked God one critical question: *Okay, God, you saw all this; you saw what happened to people like me. Where were you when all this was happening?* The Holy Spirit responded not with words, but with a vision. Nick says, "I saw Jesus. He was battered and bruised, and all he wore was a loincloth." Nick saw Roman soldiers flip Jesus over, and with the heavy whips and the scourge they begin to flog his back. He could see pieces of flesh ripped out of Jesus' back with every flogging. Nick started to scream out loud, "You are hurting him! You need to stop! Stop this!" But they continued to beat, flog, and scourge Jesus. When they stopped, they flipped Jesus over and onto a cross. They savagely drove nails into his hands and feet. Nick says he then saw a man spear Jesus in his side. Jesus screamed in pain.

In his heart Nick heard,

> This is where Jesus was. This is what happened every time your mom was saying those things in the morning before school. This is what happened every time you had to defend yourself. This is what happened every time you, your father, your father's father, and your fathers before him experienced racism. This is what happened. Know for sure that your past pain stops here. Surrender it all, and it stops here. In the past your ancestors were taken against their will to serve others. I brought you home to Africa, to the place where it started, to say that the pain and shame end here. Your son will not have to bear it; your daughter will not have to endure this; it ends here. It is done; it is finished; it is cut off; it ends here.

CHRIST-CENTERED

We have seen how the Lord empowers people of color who, like the Israelites, leave places of bondage and take their entire family, neighbors, and all of their stuff with them. These have gone further than their ancestors and have reclaimed gifts and possessions not only for themselves but also for their communities. Their lives offer us hope and some valuable lessons about how racial trauma can be processed and healed.

Before we delve into more specifics about healing racial trauma, we need to fully understand healing. What do we do when someone is broken and in need of healing? Do we believe healing should be quick, relatively pain free, and come with a guarantee? God does not fix us in this way. He wants to take us from being broken and poured out against our will to being intentionally broken of our own willfulness. Healing is not a quick fix; we are on a journey. The reality is that the painful acknowledgment of trauma and brokenness is a prerequisite to our healing and wholeness. Racism will not end, so we need God to repeatedly reveal the state of our hearts and the areas in our lives where we hurt and still need a Savior. In the midst of the trial he shows us how he is at work in us to heal our wounds.

Recently, scholar Shawn Ginwright argued for a shift to healing-centered engagement instead of trauma-informed care.[1] That departure shifts the focus from "what's wrong with you" to "what's right with you." I agree in part that a healing-centered engagement is important. But trauma-informed care rightly assumes that we've all experienced some level of trauma, so we should treat everyone in a way that promotes safety, empowerment, and healing. Ultimately, our healing journey needs to be Christ-centered, where the care, prayer, and support we receive is biblically grounded and centered on the complete work of Jesus Christ that brings hope and healing. The Lord is beyond time and space; he was there and is here. When our healing journey is Christ-centered, the Lord accompanies us as we walk through the very beginning of our pain and racial trauma. The Lord ministers healing to us through counselors, supportive groups, our families, and our communities. He then reveals "what is right with us, our families and communities," and empowers and helps us to grow in resilience. The journey of healing racial trauma first involves the internal work of addressing soul repair, reversing transgenerational trauma, telling the whole story, working through forgiveness, and post-traumatic growth. Next is the external process of rehumanizing the "other," pursuing true reconciliation, and bridging the divide.

THE INTERNAL WORK

Soul repair. When we experience a betrayal-based moral injury, a violation of moral and ethical conduct leading to disastrous consequences often without redress or justice, we need soul repair. Soul repair involves identifying how racism causes a betrayal-based moral injury that affects our faith in God, trust in self and others, discernment of right and wrong, and belief in institutions that are supposed to protect us.[2] Soul repair happens as we get clear about what happened and our true feelings about God. Soul repair involves being honest about our struggles with anger at God, ourselves, and others. As we share our moral injury with a friend, counselor, or spiritual adviser, we get help to process racial trauma. The Lord can handle our prayers of lament. When Nick shared his betrayal-based moral injury in South Africa, the depth of grief, isolation, and fear was exposed and unpacked. In prayer, we can renounce the lie that we are unimportant to God and the message we received from racial trauma that we aren't good enough.

For some racially traumatized folks, full-emersion baptism as an adult has aided in soul repair. Galatians 2:19-20 says, "I have been crucified with Christ; and it is no longer I who live, but it is Christ who lives in me. And the life I now live in the flesh I live by faith in the Son of God, who loved me and gave himself for me." There is a sense of cleansing from the past racial trauma as we are submerged in the waters and a sense of new life as we arise. When we confront our moral injury, our perceptions may be challenged about who is responsible for what, such that we have a paradigm shift about what happened and needs to happen. We then remember God's love and faithfulness and become more open each day to new experiences of his goodness and mercy. We may begin to discover the larger unfolding meaning behind what happened and what God would want us to do about it.

Healing historical and transgenerational trauma. The journey of healing racial trauma also involves confronting the trauma of past generations and its effect on the present. *Historical trauma* is said to include "disease, warfare, colonization, cultural genocide, and poverty, yet it is also a story of ongoing resistance—it is a history of devastation *and* survival."[3] In chapter one we discussed the fact that the field of epigenetics has shown that historical and *transgenerational trauma* may be passed down through the generations. But science is now backing up the fact that healing is possible. Encouraging new research has revealed a positive experience can reverse the effects of trauma transmitted to offspring.[4] How do we discover which positive experiences will repair our DNA? Positive experiences are subjective. We can have different reactions to the same situation. The one constant believers have is God, who is at work in our lives on our behalf regardless of whether our experience is positive or negative.

Our family and community stories of resilience, activism, and aspiration are important; they counter oppressive stereotypes and narratives.[5] Our stories of resistance and persistence help heal transgenerational trauma and bring to life messages of resilience and well-being.[6]

Nori's healing began as he shared his entire story with a compassionate Japanese friend. This positive experience was a turning point in Nori's life because he was able to see the real impact of his father's internment. His transgenerational trauma was exposed, and the healing path for Nori also included the way of forgiveness. Healing transgenerational trauma also involves addressing issues of bitterness and unforgiveness. Each step Nori took toward forgiving his dad of the bad that occurred and the good that didn't diminished the trauma he carried until it entirely lifted.

The entire story. When people of color experience racial trauma, we tell ourselves a story that is incomplete, competing, or limiting. It is not uncommon for us to remain silent about our family history. The problem is that when we avoid the bad stuff, we often don't share the good things either. When we face our untold stories, our feelings get unblocked, and we are free to tell our truth. This happened for me. As I wrote this book I was confronted by how I glossed over the racial trauma I experienced at Roslindale High. While interviewing schoolmates I was reminded of how terrifying it was for me to see angry White faces spewing hate and the sight and sound of rocks and bottles thrown at the windows of my school bus. The bottom line is that we have to be truthful. It takes courage and strength to look for and look at where we are hurting and broken. No matter how much we want to be healed, we can't make ourselves feel our pain if we are numbing it, but we can stop doing the things that keep us from feeling. We can lay our defenses, addictions, and self-saving strategies at the foot of the cross and allow our emotions to surface.

When we are struggling, listening prayer can be helpful in identifying what we are feeling and why. We can place our hand on our heart and ask the Lord to help locate any troubling sensations in our body. Often this allows us to get in touch with how we really feel. As we pray, the Lord meets us in the rawness of our trauma and reveals what the stress or pain is trying to communicate. The Lord can identify the source of the toxic racial trauma and the means of releasing it from our bodies. Carla found music and liturgical dance to be helpful in accessing her feelings and removing the traumatic stress she carried in her body. She has learned how shallow her breathing is when she is experiencing rage or anxiety. Carla takes several slow, deep breaths and counts to ten while breathing in through her nostrils and out through her mouth.

Sometimes we may have an increase in trauma symptoms after getting in touch with our pain. But this can be an opportunity to learn how to sit with our emotions and allow them to come and go. If we go with the flow of our feelings as they intensify and decrease, we can learn how to accept ourselves as vulnerable and feeling people who can process our racial trauma without it overtaking us. I've found nonjudgmental writing in a journal, as well as artwork, to be a great way to pour out my feelings as a prayer. Feelings are not facts, but they are messengers trying to tell us something. The apostle Paul reminds us to "take every thought captive to obey Christ" (2 Corinthians 10:5). Sometimes we need to take captive the limiting story that we keep telling ourselves about who we and our people are and what we don't have.

When we uncover and share our entire story, we start to see big and small things to be grateful for, and we are reminded that God has not forgotten us. Over time we learn to fully inhabit our story because Jesus offers hope, blessings, and resilience along the way.

Working through forgiveness. First John 4:19-20 reminds us, "We love because he first loved us. Whoever claims to love God yet hates a brother or sister is a liar. For whoever does not love their brother and sister, whom they have seen, cannot love God, whom they have not seen. And he has given us this command: Anyone who loves God must also love their brother and sister" (NIV). These are hard words. Olga Botcharova, a peacebuilding activist, has outlined how our relational path leads toward either reconciliation or revenge. Like Nori, each person in this book had to decide which path to take. The steps of revenge begin with a racist incident, and then the resulting racial trauma is left unaddressed. Botcharova explains that our unprocessed feelings of "grief and fear only intensify feelings of anger and hatred directed towards the perpetrators and towards anything associated with him or her, ranging from family members and neighbors to members of the perpetrator's gender and ethnic, religious and political group. When this happens, the perpetrator is dehumanized and we the victim are stuck in a cycle of revenge."[7]

One meaning of the Greek word for forgiveness is "to release from one's grasp." When our grief, fear, anger, and hatred turn into unforgiveness, we are grasping the scruff of the neck of the one who hurt us and saying, "I will not let you go until you have paid for what you have done." Some of us harbor anger that has become rage turned inward, and we inadvertently take revenge on ourselves. For years some of us have been holding tightly to our enemy, and unforgiveness has become like an old friend that we walk with every day.

Some of us feel stuck, unable or unwilling to release our grasp and forgive because we think unforgiveness is a neutral position. I used to think, *If I don't forgive this person, I just don't forgive them. It's not going to kill them. It's not going to hurt me. We are just not going to have a relationship. It's not going to affect anything.* I found that this is a lie. Our decision not to forgive actually means we are siding with the enemy of our souls; it is not a neutral place.

The danger Olga Botcharova describes is that we may falsely believe "that relief from pain can only occur if its source or cause is punished or destroyed. When the justice system fails to accomplish this, or the punishment received by the perpetrator is considered inadequate, the victims might become prone to perform the act of 'justified aggression,' thus completing the cycle of revenge." God wants to heal us, but if we refuse to release our grip on unforgiveness, we will miss the true redemption available to us in and through Christ. Botcharova warns us that taking revenge will never facilitate healing. When a victim performs an act of "justified" aggression or punishment, "the cycle of violence is completed, with the roles now reversed. The former perpetrator now feels victimized, seeks revenge, and, finally, strikes again when an opportunity occurs."[8]

Author Claudia Black tells us, "Forgiving is not forgetting; it is remembering and letting go."[9] Yet few can honestly say that forgiveness comes easy, particularly in situations where we have been deeply hurt. We struggle to forgive for many reasons. There is the lie that says forgiveness costs too much and is too painful. We also tell ourselves we will receive nothing if we forgive and all we will have done is to let that person off the hook. This is not what true forgiveness is. When we forgive, we are not saying that what they did to us was okay. We are not saying that they are free to do again what they have done to us. We are not quickly dismissing what happened, how we feel about it, or how it affected our hearts. Our forgiveness actually frees us to move on with our lives regardless of what the other person does. Restoration of the future is the goal of forgiveness, not just handing out punishment, which locks everything into the past.

Ephesians 4:32 says, "Be kind to one another, tenderhearted, forgiving one another, as God in Christ has forgiven you." How do we forgive? We can start where we are and ask God for the desire and ability to forgive. We can choose to obey the command to forgive. As we pray and confess what was done to us, we also release our abusers to the Lord and no longer act as judge, jury, and executioner. We are able to forgive because we have the assurance that Jesus assumed our racial trauma on the cross. If speaking is difficult, you can write whatever you are holding onto as an act of forgiveness and symbolically give it to the Lord by shredding or burning the paper. The Lord also cleanses us from the effect of the wounding and the unforgiveness we've held onto.

The Holy Spirit affirms our freedom with peace and joy despite the circumstances. On the cross Jesus said, "Father, forgive them, for they do not know what they are doing." Jesus not only models love and forgiveness but empowers us to forgive, frees us, and restores our relationships. Jesus assures us that he will help us attain freedom and stay free. He has given us the Comforter, the Holy Spirit. Once we know how much of our brokenness and trauma has been healed because of Christ's love for us, we are able to forgive and love "the other."

Post-traumatic growth. Like Joseph before his brothers in Genesis 50:20, we can also proclaim, "Even though you intended to do harm to me, God intended it for good, in order to preserve a numerous people, as he is doing today." Researchers have found that trauma can be transformative. Post-traumatic growth (PTG) acknowledges "the resilience and growth that can occur following a traumatic event whereby the individual derives meaning from an incident that caused suffering to transcend the trauma." Outcomes of PTG can include a greater sense of compassion and value toward the other, enhanced personal relationships, and an overall appreciation of life, including an emphasis on resiliency.[10] May our eyes and ears be opened to the fact that the Lord is constantly speaking to us through his Word, people, and experiences. The Lord helps us transcend trauma and always works on our behalf to empower and build resilience within us. God has given us the Holy Spirit—with his peace, grace, and power—so we can tell our people where hope and healing are found.

THE EXTERNAL WORK

Rehumanizing the other. Dr. Botcharova writes, "Acknowledging the pain felt by those on the opposite side of a conflict may allow the victim to gradually develop compassion towards 'the other' and, thus, begin the process of re-humanizing the perpetrator."[11] I experienced this process after moving to the North Shore of Boston. We spent our Sundays church hopping until we landed at a multiracial and multicultural church full of millennials in Cambridge. It was the same denomination as our vibrant home church in Johannesburg. Our new senior pastor suggested that we connect with Brian and Sara, a young couple who like us had a heart for emotional-healing ministry. We invited the couple to our place for dinner, and as we shared our life stories and discussed race and racism, we found significant commonalities. Brian shared his life and faith journey, which included a Catholic grandmother who was prominent in Boston's antibusing movement. Brian was stunned when he learned of his grandmother's past. He said, "It was hard for me to reconcile the woman, loved and respected by her family, the church, and community being the same woman giving hate-filled speeches."

During the court-ordered busing era in Boston, many White parents in Brian's community refused to allow their kids to be bused to a school in a Black neighborhood. Those who could afford it enrolled their kids in a private or Catholic school. Brian said, "Many of the kids were kept at home, and hundreds if not thousands went uneducated." Almost an entire generation was left without high school diplomas. When those kids grew up, many were equipped only to work menial jobs, do contract work, or get a job with the city. While some studied and passed the General Education Development (GED) test to get their high school diplomas, others spent their days loitering, drinking, and engaging in petty theft.

As I heard the story from the other side, I realized how unaware I was of the impact that busing had on the poor and working-class White communities of South Boston, Dorchester, Hyde Park, and Charlestown. Although many success stories came out of the busing era, Ray Flynn, former mayor of Boston, noted, "You can walk around Roxbury, you can walk around South Boston, you'll see many victims of the busing decision that didn't allow them to go to school or get an education that they needed and deserved."[12] We could say it was their fault. However, the reality is the kids did not make the choice on their own. They faced the consequences of decisions made by their parents.

One of the consequences of generational racism is that it taints everyone. I wonder how different things would have been if Boston's poor White, Black, and Brown communities recognized that they had more commonalities than differences and demanded that the city choose justice for all. I don't know if things will ever change for Brian's family. I don't know how his family feels about Black and Brown folks, but what I do know is that a generation later some things have changed. The neighborhoods that were formerly no-go places now have different racial and ethnic groups mingling. Most importantly, Brian and Sara's son now attends a church where he knows and sees many Black, Brown, and White folks worshiping the same God. Life together can be a hard and often messy journey; we will undoubtedly offend one another, but we will persevere.

That night at our dining table I was reminded that alongside people of color there are White allies actively combating White supremacy and pursuing reconciliation and social justice. That night I had a glimpse of Martin Luther King Jr.'s dream that "one day the sons of former slaves and the sons of former slave owners will be able to sit down together at a table of brotherhood."[13] As our dinner ended, we prayed for one another, and a spark of hope was reignited within me.

Liza experienced another rehumanization of the other. Her healing journey took a surprising turn after she took a DNA test. Although she knew her heritage contained European, indigenous, and African blood, she was stunned by the percentages of each. Liza always identified as being Brown, the colonized instead of the colonizer, the enslaved rather than the slave trader. Her DNA test revealed a much higher percentage of Iberian blood than she expected. She's come to terms with the fact that like other people of color she carries significant Caucasian DNA. This solidified a call for her to stop demonizing the colonizer and instead fight for justice in a way that maintains the *imago Dei* (image of God) in everyone, even the perpetrator.

True reconciliation. The next step toward true racial reconciliation, according to Professor Miroslav Volf, involves repentance and repair.[14] This is a challenge because much of what has been done and said in the name of racial reconciliation has missed this point. People of color have received apologies, but true reconciliation involves the perpetrator's personal and public apology to people of color for the past and present harm. Also, *repentance* must include a commitment to stop all actions of injustice and oppression and to repair any damage done. If we want true reconciliation that is flourishing, then *repair* is essential; without it the apology and repentance can feel shallow. In Luke 19 we learn about repair from Zacchaeus, the chief tax collector, an agent for state-sanctioned systemic oppression. After Jesus invites himself to Zacchaeus's home, Zacchaeus is convicted and tells Jesus, "Look, Lord! Here and now I give half of my possessions to the poor, and if I have cheated anybody out of anything, I will pay back four times the amount" (v. 8 NIV). People of color are still waiting, and some are demanding repair and reparations for the damage that racism has caused to individuals, families, and communities. The Shinnecock would prefer that their stolen land is returned; if not, then they desire monetary reparation. If there is any hope for true and full reconciliation, then repair must happen on a macro- or microlevel. Repair can take different forms. An example of macro-level repair of systemic injustice is the financial reparations that Japanese Americans received because of the internment.

The closest that America came to reparations for slavery was after the Civil War when Major General William Sherman signed Special Field Order No. 15. It promised each formerly enslaved family forty acres and a mule. However, President Andrew Johnson, Lincoln's successor, overturned the order in 1865. Other attempts at repair, such as the Voting Rights Act and Affirmative Action, which aimed to increase minority participation in voting, hiring, and education, constantly have been under siege. Repair means little if the injustice it attempts to rectify is undermined.

On a microlevel, repair between individuals can occur, such as when Granddaddy James complained about not getting full price for his crops and a White farmer pulled Granddaddy aside and told him to place the produce on the back of his pickup truck. The White farmer was actually engaging in repair when he upheld the dignity of Granddaddy James and sold the produce as his own so Granddaddy could get full price. Recently a White actress added a clause in her contract that her African American female costar would receive equal pay. People of color may also have to repent and repair any damage, justified or not, that we've caused by our response to racism. True reconciliation occurs after we have worked through forgiveness, repentance, and repair. The perpetrators' repentance and repair, as well as our forgiveness, are acts that can free us all from our guilt and resentment so we can all turn toward pursuing and embracing restored relationships across the racial dividing lines.

Bridging the divide. Ephesians 2:13-14 says, "But now in Christ Jesus you who once were far away have been brought near by the blood of Christ. For he himself is our peace, who has made the two groups one and has destroyed the barrier, the dividing wall of hostility" (NIV). Whether we see it or not, Jesus did a complete work, reconciling all racial, ethnic, and gender groups. He destroyed the dividing wall; it's up to us to stop rebuilding it.

One of the hallmarks of the early church was the unlikely combination of its members. Rome once was a powerful, diverse, multicultural society, with haves and have-nots, the mainstreamed and the marginalized, important and common folk. People tended to hang with their own kind, but what distinguished Christian community is that it cut across all sorts of dividing lines rigidly enforced elsewhere. These folks who came together in community and relationship had no business being together. They did not decide to get together, but were brought together by the Spirit and were given a vision of the possible by those who had walked with Jesus. As Jesus interacted with people, he met them where they were. He brought to light the real issue or need and called forth the real child of God. The common bond between all is Jesus. He affirmed diversity in his ministry, at the time of his death, after his resurrection, and then at Pentecost.

In South Africa, when Nick encountered the Lord in listening prayer, the White men in his small group were profoundly affected, and precious time of confession and forgiveness was initiated. One man lay in the fetal position in a corner, and the others were sobbing. The leader of the group choked up and kept repeating, "I never knew. I never knew." Another man said, "I'm so sorry. I'm so sorry." The men were awakened to the reality of how the sinful structures of racism wounded all of them. The men asked Nick for forgiveness for their denial of racism while benefiting from the legacy of apartheid. Nick was able to forgive the men, and as they prayed for one another that day, all of them were freed.

In 2 Corinthians 1:3-4 we are told, "Praise be to the God and Father of our Lord Jesus Christ, the Father of compassion and the God of all comfort, who comforts us in all our troubles, so that we can comfort those in any trouble with the comfort we ourselves receive from God" (NIV). It's time to share your story of struggle and healing from racial trauma while on the road to resilience. Your story may bring hope and healing to those still bound by sadness, rage, fear, fatigue, shame, silence, and addiction.

REFLECTION AND PRAYER PROMPTS

1. How can you make Jesus the center of your healing journey?

2. Are your gifts or abilities locked up because of racial trauma? As a prayer to God, write what you want to reclaim and ask the Lord how to do it.

3. We are forgiven. Now we are to forgive. Take a couple of deep breaths and sit silently and listen. Identify someone you need to forgive and get him or her clearly in mind. Take a sheet of paper and put that person's name at the top. Now ask yourself if you are willing to forgive this person totally, absolutely, and unconditionally. If so, in prayer, as you hand the person over to God, say, "I forgive you and release you to Jesus."

4. Take a few moments and write down all the ways God has directly or indirectly met your needs.

5. How will you bring the good news of healing and freedom to others?

CHAPTER TEN

RESILIENCE

Their life shall become like a watered garden,
and they shall never languish again.

JEREMIAH 31:12

The first time we ran a healing support group, it was at an inner-city church in Boston. We spent months advertising and then followed up with extensive interviews of applicants. The final group members were Black, White, Latino, Latina, and Asian women and men with professions ranging from supermarket bagger to pediatrician. Some of them came from the community, a few lived over the border in Rhode Island, and others came in from the suburbs of Boston.

The first meeting started with a high level of anticipation as the members arrived and took a seat on a wooden pew in the sanctuary. We began with a beautiful time of worship to help us to focus our attention on the Lord as the source of healing. The teaching for the evening focused on the question that Jesus posed to the man lying by the Beth-zatha pool (John 5). When Jesus saw the man lying there and learned that he had been in this condition for thirty-eight years, he asked, "Do you want to be made well?" (v. 6). This seems like an unnecessary, even cruel, question, but it was actually an important one.

This was the same question we asked the group members to consider in their small groups. My small group's chairs were arranged in a circle, and we had one extra chair. I told the women, "This seat is for the Lord, who is present with us even if we can't see him." One by one the women shared what had brought them there, and they poured out their pain. At 9:30 p.m. my group was the first to wrap up, and the members and I went to the sanctuary. As I was coming down the stairs, Nick was going up, and he whispered, "How was it?" I nodded, and we gave each other a high-five as we passed. I reached the bottom of the stairs, and as I walked toward the sanctuary, the double doors of the church suddenly burst open. A young Black man stumbled into the entrance and collapsed. There was a drive-by shooting nearby, and the man was the target. He had been shot in the leg. The police arrived within minutes, and the EMTs stabilized him and moved him to an awaiting ambulance.

As the other small groups ended, the police ushered the members into the sanctuary while forensics did their investigation. It was hard to fathom how our church had just hosted an incredible night of healing and now it was a crime scene. There we sat, sang worship songs, prayed for the young man, and waited. I could see the fear on some faces. This experience was foreign and shocking to them. As we were praying, I sensed that the Lord wanted to impart a deeper meaning. I told the participants, "I can totally understand why you'd want to drop out of this group. But I believe that God is doing something here. You have to ask yourself if you are willing to take the risk. Many of you have experiences or have taken risks of one kind or another throughout your life that were as dangerous as a drive-by."

I said, "It may not look like it, but I believe that this group is an opportunity for you to choose life. It is up to you." During the week I called each member. Some were struggling with returning;

however, by the next meeting they all returned. At our final session, one by one group members testified about the impact of that first night and how their decision to get well altered their lives.

Jesus asks us the same question he asked the man by the pool: "Do you want to be made well?" The fact that you have begun this healing journey is a testament that you also want to get well. The question now is, How do we stay well and become more resilient? As people of color living in America (and around the world) continue to be impacted by racism and racial trauma, we will need God's grace, stamina, and resilience to stay well. Whether we are minding our own business or are the intended target, we are all at risk from racism, which is like the spray of bullets during a drive-by. We try to get well and stay well, but at any point there may be a random racist action, a drive-by followed by injustice and inaction that assaults our personhood. We can learn how to stay well and build resilience as we focus on what God has done, what he is doing now, what you can do, what we can do, and the resurrection.

WHAT HAS GOD DONE?

Forgetfulness is one of the main issues the Israelites struggled with in the desert. Every day and night the Lord met their needs in small and significant ways, yet they quickly forgot or failed to fully appreciate all that he had done. We are no different. Failure to remember invites fear, arrogance, and pride. We forget how we were healed in the first place and who sustains our healing. Pride and fear often come before a relapse into old, dysfunctional ways of reacting and responding. When our perspective is off, our faith in God diminishes, and we become overwhelmed with worry, negative thoughts, and emotions. In this state, after a racially charged incident, resilience or bouncing back becomes difficult.

One October day I watched the morning news report of migrants threatened with force if they sought asylum in the United States. I also saw the supermarket where a White supremacist shot and killed Black senior citizens Maurice Stallard and Vickie Jones. Then on Saturday morning another White supremacist burst into the Tree of Life Synagogue and killed eleven Jewish congregants. I prayed a prayer of lament. I sobbed and railed like David in the psalms. I felt the pain and the weight of the news stories along with the stories of the folks in this book. As I cried out to the Lord, he reminded me of his love and sacrifice for us all. Everything that he has done for us emanates from his heart of love. Jesus demonstrated that love when he did his complete work on the cross, forgiving our sin, redeeming our lives, and restoring our relationship with God and others. Jesus has conquered sin, death, racism, and injustice.

Because we are prone to forgetfulness, it is essential to write down and remember what God has done and how our lives have changed. In the Bible there are genealogies and stories of family history over generations. These stories are like genograms that record the tragedy, triumphs, and resilience in a family line. In the same way, the Lord calls us to remember our whole story. As we retell it, humility surfaces as we become aware of God's faithfulness over time. Psalm 129:2-4 reminds us,

"Often have they attacked me from my youth,
    yet they have not prevailed against me.
The plowers plowed on my back;
    they made their furrows long."
The LORD is righteous;
    he has cut the cords of the wicked.

We now stand among the multitudes who pray, keep the faith, and persevere against all the odds because we trust that God has the final say.

There have been countless times when it was evident that the Lord has the final say. It was evident when my Great-Granddaddy took his neighbor, the White farmer, to court and won. It was evident when slavery was abolished. It was evident when the Civil Rights Act of 1964 passed, making discrimination based on race, color, religion, gender, or national origin illegal. It was evident in Carol and Ed's sixty-year marriage. In every generation there is evidence that because of Jesus, healing, resilience building, racial reconciliation, and justice are not pipe dreams.

WHAT IS GOD DOING NOW?

As we continue on our journey of healing, Jesus repeatedly asks, "Do you want to stay well?"

This happened to me a year after the 2016 presidential election as the racial tension in the country escalated and each day insults and assaults were coming from the White House. The signs of unprocessed trauma were evident in my responses, which ranged from silence to oversharing and from survivor guilt to being easily triggered by the latest news cycle. Sometimes I found myself crying for an unknown reason. Psalm 119:81-82 spoke to my emotional state and plea to the Lord:

My soul languishes for your salvation;
    I hope in your word.
My eyes fail with watching for your promise;
    I ask, "When will you comfort me?"

I spent one evening in 2017 in prayer asking the Lord to comfort and help me to better understand what was going on in my own heart. I felt I'd get clarity through listening prayer. Jesus modeled this by his two-way communication with God the Father. The question I pondered was how willing and far would I go to hear from God and get healed. In order to experience and learn more about a type of listening prayer that I found transformative, I agreed to a three-hour journey to a church in a small, mostly White town on the New Hampshire border. My friend Dorothy called me brave. I called myself desperate.

Two middle-aged White women were my listening-prayer counselors. They warmly welcomed me, and I felt this was a safe place to seek God. After telling them why I was there, we prayed and listened for the Holy Spirit to reveal the heart of the matter. One of the counselors asked, "Are you battling with anger?" I paused and then asked them, "Do you really want me to go there?" They said yes, so I fought back tears and shared all that was troubling me. Then I had a disturbing thought. I wondered aloud if people of color woke up on November 9, 2016, and silently questioned if we were left as orphans. Did God really care about the oppression of people of color, widows, orphans, or foreigners? The prayer counselors were weepy as they pondered how the choices made by some had unintentionally or not burned bridges and helped build dividing walls of hostility between the races.

I've had plenty of time since that meeting to think about the lessons learned then and from ongoing encounters with Jesus in prayer. One significant thing is Jesus' assurance of John 14:18-19: "I will not leave you orphaned; I am coming to you. In a little while the world will no longer see me, but you will see me; because I live, you also will live." God has not left us as orphans. Our hope and faith are kept alive through the Scriptures. We know that God sees us, goes out of the way to listen to our whole story, opens our eyes, and enables us to stand. The Lord weeps with us, forgives us, and imparts hope and healing in darkness and death. God cares for and about people of color and is with us before, during, and after every racially traumatic experience. Gradually, we begin to see mounting evidence of what God is doing in and through our lives, and we become grateful. We see evidence when a just judge presides in a court, when police brutality leads to conviction, and when a person of color runs for political office and wins. We see it when people of color and White allies expose and oppose systemic oppression, such as mass incarceration, and when poverty is alleviated. We see evidence that God is at work when a church or ministry, no longer White-centered, is Christ-centered, reflecting the full diversity in Christ's church.

WHAT CAN WE DO?

We are in an age of outrage, because for far too long folks have been silenced. Righteous indignation is appropriate, but it can't stop at outrage. It has to lead to prayer and positive action. We start in prayer because that is where positive transformation starts. Racial trauma is real, and our negative response to it is understandable but sometimes not consistent with our values. If we are to be more resilient, we must identify and be clear about our moral compass— what we really value. This is not about what we are supposed to value. When we take an honest look at our lives, we will see what we actually believe and prioritize, and where we spend most of our time, talents, and money. If we know what we value, it's easy to see if we are walking in agreement with what is important to us. If we discover that we are operating contrary to our values, we can choose to repent, no longer compromise, and then realign our values.

Sometimes we are triggered and find our hair on fire because of the latest racist Tweet or Facebook post that compromises or challenges our core values or identity. If we take a moment and slow down, we may see we have options and can respond in a way that builds resilience. That trigger may be a teacher in disguise shedding light on an area within or outside of us that should be attended to.

Soul care. Entertainer Lena Horne said, "It's not the load that breaks you down, it's the way you carry it."[1] How do you take care of yourself in these challenging times? What do you do when once again you're carrying chronic racial trauma from having to hold your story when it's not seen or validated? As you grow more rooted in the knowledge of God's love and care, you become more open to love and care for your soul just as you would care for a dear friend.

Soul care should be holistic, involving our spiritual, emotional, relational, physical, and vocational lives. When you are engaging in healthy soul care, you know when and how to rest, destress, expose injustice, and advocate for your needs and those of others. Old practices that helped our ancestors to cope and heal have been discarded; we should now reengage them. All of these help us to build resilience. It's also time to develop methods of soul care that builds on the past, the present, and our resilience, and recognizes that in Christ we are and have more than enough.

Spiritual. When you are distracted and flat in your connection to the Lord, it is a warning sign that something is off. Have you had an experience that has caused a moral injury? Has it caused you to question the goodness of God? If this is the case, your relationship with God may be affected and in need of soul repair. Soul repair begins as you prioritize your relationship with the Lord, not just to share what's on your heart but also to hear what is on his. It also helps to regularly read the Scriptures and other inspirational books. When you take a sabbath day of rest each week, it is an act of trust to set aside your work and fear and place them in God's capable hands while you rest. When you are attentive to the Lord your perspective becomes clearer, fear is reduced, and you're less likely to get caught up in unnecessary drama. It is essential that you worship from your heart; do not relegate your culture to the margins. Worship and pray in your own language and in your own ways. During slavery, Negro spirituals like "Wade in the Water" were thought to be solely about water baptism, but it was a song of faith, perseverance, hope, and freedom. It actually was a coded message that instructed the enslaved people that the safest way of escape was through the river.

Professor James Cone wrote about the significance of Sunday church service during the lynching period: "Black Christians spoke back in song, sermon, and prayer against the faceless, merciless, apocalyptic vengefulness of the massed white mob, to show that trouble and sorrow would not determine our final meaning. African Americans embraced the story of Jesus, the crucified Christ whose death they claimed paradoxically gave them life."[2] The Holy Spirit reminded me that the marginalized in society and persons of color mostly attended to Jesus as he journeyed to the cross. Simon of Cyrene, a man of color, a foreigner from North Africa, helped carry the cross for Jesus. Mary, Jesus' mother, and Mary Magdalene, both women with no social or political clout, were there with Jesus. John, an ordinary fisherman, was at the foot of the cross. Joseph of Arimathea, the only one who had social status, placed his status at risk by burying Jesus, a convicted felon. People of color are people of the cross and of the resurrection. Today, ethnic churches, gospel music, and the exploration of the early church encourage the same hope, healing, and sanctuary that our ancestors had. You can also reclaim your place in the story of Christ's church.

Emotional. When you choose to stay well, you accept that change and challenges are part of life. So, you can be totally alive rather than living in self-focused detached numbness. Racism and microaggressions will still occur, but you can change how you interpret and respond to them. You can look out for signs of racial battle fatigue (for example, building a wall around your heart to prevent hurt from happening again). When you try to shut out the bad stuff, you may also cut off your heart from feeling all the good things God has provided. You are free, a real person with real needs; give them and the needs of others you can't meet to the Lord. Jesus can help you to define and maintain your boundaries, such as choosing when you want to talk about or respond to race and racism. Boundaries prevent your heart from being an exposed space anyone can walk over or exploit for selfish reasons. The Lord is teaching us how to be healthy and balanced people who can say no without being manipulated by social media or other people. You can discern when to extend yourself safely. Ask the Lord to show you how.

Relational. Jesus must be at the center of your struggle and desire for connection. When you rest in him and allow him to work in your relationships, they become sacred ground out of which healthy connections will emerge. Because life can be a battle, you especially need other people. Nick's parents, like many immigrants and Southern folks, grew up on a farm. They retained peace of mind by owning a house and a little piece of land to garden. Relatives pooled their funds, bought multiple family dwellings, and raised their families in community. For some of you the breakdown of family and community has meant that you've had to go elsewhere for safer spaces to revive and recharge.

I once heard someone say these safer spaces where people of color gather are unnecessary and divisive. My response: White people have exclusively White gatherings all the time, even on Sundays, and no one has an issue with it. I believe safer spaces for people of color actually help us to mutually support each other, revive, and persevere in the pursuit of racial reconciliation. Bethel AME Church was that for my family. And at the church we now attend we've found similar support. We attend a monthly "family dinner" where African Americans, those from the African diaspora, and those in biracial relationships connect and share a meal. The gathering is free from any pretense or performance. It is liberating. Supportive environments like this can be a sanctuary or a place that offers protection from the "ravages of racism."[3] At home, at work, and even online we can create these healing relationships and communities that help us to be more resilient.

Physical. In many of our families, folk medicine helped keep us healthy. My mother was an early adopter of herbal medication, some passed down from her mother. Momae's bitter-tasting tincture kept us healthy throughout the Boston winters. When our bodies are healthy, we are in a better position to fight the racial trauma retained in our bodies. There are many ways to release that stress in order to stay well—resting, engaging in creative and expressive arts, physical recreation such as painting, writing, jogging, walking, biking, or swimming. Sometimes you know something is off but are unaware that you're carrying racial trauma. Periodically check in with your body, looking for tension, stress, or pain. When this happens for Carla, she prays and soon senses God's comforting arms of love around her. As she hugs herself, she is reminded that God deeply cares for her mind, body, and soul.

Vocation. Ephesians 2:10 reminds us, "We are God's handiwork, created in Christ Jesus to do good works, which God prepared in advance for us to do" (NIV). The "flaming arrows" that Paul talks about in Ephesians 6 are not randomly fired in your direction. It is not an accident that you are called to proclaim the gospel or to be a prophetic voice, yet you have an addiction or events happened in life that robbed you of your voice. For many of us the consequence of racism, family, and societal dysfunction is a profound lack of confidence and a nagging inability to take risks. Or we experience restless activism, an inability to be still and know that our Lord is God; thus we are close to burning out. If the evil one has not destroyed a sense of purpose in your life, he is trying to distract you from fully engaging in it now. And if that does not work, he will try to delay the recognition of your purpose. But the Lord proclaims, "Surely I know the plans I have for you . . . plans for your welfare and not for harm, to give you a future with hope. Then when you call upon me and come and pray to me, I will hear you" (Jeremiah 29:11-12). Despite how racism has tried to hijack your future each day, you can get support and intentionally choose to take one small step toward your future.

LOVING OUR NEIGHBORS

When a Pharisee asked Jesus which commandment in the law is the greatest, Jesus said to him, "'You shall love the Lord your God with all your heart, and with all your soul, and with all your mind.' This is the greatest and first commandment. And a second is like it: 'You shall love your neighbor as yourself.' On these two commandments hang all the law and the prophets" (Matthew 22:37-40). Literally everything in the Bible is encompassed in those verses. These verses are foundational to true reconciliation. We love God, and in turn we are to love and pray for our neighbor, our friend, our spouse, even our enemy in the same way that we do for ourselves. Where does this love come from? Its origin is supernatural; God gives us the grace to love even the unlovable.

Yet we often find ourselves behaving to the contrary. We give to others to get. We quickly become impatient, unkind, self-seeking, and angry, especially when with folk we don't agree with. I've asked myself, *Why is it so hard to put God first and to let his love flow through me so I can better love my neighbor and even my enemy?* Reconciled relationships are core to who we are as believers, and yet they are so difficult to obtain and maintain, especially when race is involved. Because people of color continue to have experiences that are unkind, unloving, and brutal, we've created our own ways to manage life in a majority-White context. At times we've connected with White folks from the place of fear, suspicion, or anger because we never know when racism will rear its ugly head.

Racism is like the elephant in the room that we pretend is not there. However, we now see that it's enormous and we're tripping over it. How do we get rid of it? If we try to move it alone, it won't budge. It's going to take a large number of folks of all races undergoing a heart change, sharing our stories and our lives, and challenging false narratives. If we all speak up and engage in small and large acts that pursue love, peace, and justice, we can dismantle the systemic structures that promote racism, xenophobia, White supremacy, and privilege. The apostle Paul says, "The weapons of our warfare are not merely human, but they have divine power to destroy strongholds"(2 Corinthians 10:4). Fredrick Buechner writes about the power of love: "It is the most powerful because it alone can conquer that final and most impregnable stronghold which is the human heart."[4] Our life is not to be passive or reactive—we are in an ongoing war against racism, but we war in prayer and with love.

While we would like to play it safe in our cross-racial relationships, the Lord imparts wisdom about when and with whom to risk and be more authentic. Difficult relationships should push us into a closer relationship with God, who will help us respond more like Jesus. Martin Luther King Jr. spoke about how we are to "fight for justice while loving the one doing the injustice." It is not easy for people of color to live in the tension of having dear friends who are White while also having some of our most profound pain occurring at the hands of White people. Jesus spoke of our long-suffering and cries for justice when he said, "Will not God grant justice to his chosen ones who cry to him day and night? Will he delay long in helping them? I tell you, he will quickly grant justice to them." Yet I believe it's not only about what God will do. Jesus pointedly asks us, "And yet, when the Son of Man comes, will he find faith on earth?" (Luke 18:7-8). I believe justice is also secured as our faith is conjoined with works. In 1 Corinthians 15:58, Paul encourages us to be "steadfast, immovable, always excelling in the work of the Lord, because you know that in the Lord your labor is not in vain."

We are to prioritize the pursuit of a God-breathed vision for a new culture that values love, true peace, and justice. While healthy relationships with those of our own racial or ethnic group are essential, we will need to cross our racial divisions to receive the full blessings of that new vision and culture. Proverbs 27:17 says, "Iron sharpens iron, and one person sharpens the wits of another." It's not always about what White folks have to share. People of color actually have a lot to teach privileged White folks about resilience, resourcefulness, and living faithfully while under duress. We all have something that will benefit the other. When we are at our best, we are different people groups existing in the same space while continually learning how to get along and having constructive conversations about making our lives and this country better for everyone. Dietrich Bonhoeffer, a German pastor and theologian, wrote, "We are not to simply bandage the wounds of victims beneath the wheels of injustice, we are to drive a spoke into the wheel itself."[5] This will require people of color and White folks empowered by the Holy Spirit to drive a spoke in the wheel that will alleviate fear, ensure safety, address racism and injustice, and dismantle the systems and ideologies that keep us apart. I know it's possible; I've seen it. You have read about some of these in this book, both people of color and White folks who are their allies. They have made a commitment to link arms and to stop the wheels of injustice from spinning.

RESURRECTION

You've read about the resilience of the resurrection plant (see chapter seven). I experienced a similar lesson while at the Legacy Museum in Montgomery. Inside, a wall of shelves is lined with hundreds of large sealed jars. Every jar is labeled with the name of a lynching victim and the location and date of the lynching. Inside each jar are soil and possible traces of DNA collected from the confirmed site of the lynching. This area is like a mausoleum where we remember and honor the dead, and yet there is life. Despite what seems like the absence of sustenance, tiny seedlings have sprouted in some of the jars. These seedlings remind me of people of color. We are more than resilient—we are miracles. In the midst of our tragedy and trauma we work, thrive, and struggle, and the Lord continuously saves and brings grace, new life, beauty, and justice.

In John 11:25-26 Jesus says, "I am the resurrection and the life. Those who believe in me, even though they die, will live, and everyone who lives and believes in me will never die. Do you believe this?" Our resilience grows as we live and love as if this life is not the end of our story. It is written that Bryan Stevenson "looked at the jars of soil and said, 'We can grow something with this, we can create something with this that has new meaning.' That's because while soil may surround us in death, it also is the place to plant seeds of hope for a new beginning."[6] Ecclesiastes 11:6 encourages us to do that very thing: "In the morning sow your seed, and at evening do not let your hands be idle; for you do not know which will prosper, this or that, or whether both alike will be good." Therefore, we pray by faith, live like we're heaven bound, and get to work scattering our seeds. Last, we receive encouragement from Psalm 126:5-6:

> May those who sow in tears
> reap with shouts of joy.
> Those who go out weeping,
> bearing the seed for sowing,
> shall come home with shouts of joy,
> carrying their sheaves.

REFLECTION AND PRAYER PROMPTS

1. How can you grow in resilience?

2. Pray about a plan for your soul care. Write your plan and get support to implement it.

3. How will you drive a spoke into the wheel of injustice?

4. Pray about how you might engage in activism.

ACKNOWLEDGMENTS

This book would not be possible without the Lord opening the way and the words to bring it to life.

I am forever grateful for this and the support of Nicholas Rowe, the love of my life, and Jonathan and Alexia, the best adult children and cheerleaders. Your love and prayers help me to soar and give me a place to call home.

To my American and South African family of intercessors; especially my sister circle—Paulea Mooney-McCoy, Sabrina Gray, Carla Booker, Val Copeland, Natasha Andrews, Pam Christiansen, Dorothy Greco, Louise Walker, Jolly Mokorosi, Phumzile Mthethwa, Gillian Rowe, Hope Mabry, Maxine Jafta, Gail Musikavanhu, Sherry Golden, and Linda Diana Scott—thank you for lifting me up and praying this book into being.

Thank you to Liza Cagua-Koo, Caleb McCoy, Nick and Jonathan Rowe, Carla Booker, and all who gave me the honor of sharing your untold stories of faith, struggle, and resilience. Your lives challenge and inspire my faith.

A special thank you to Uncle Edward Wise and Auntie Barbara Singh for unlocking our family history.

To my siblings, Kwame, Stephanie, Makeda, Salahaldin, Ernest, Robert, Rynel, Yolanda, Tony, and Aisha, you are testimonies of the strength and love of Jesus and our Momae. I am grateful for our shared story.

To my editor, Cindy Bunch, and publisher, InterVarsity Press, it has been a delight to work with you. Your insightful and indispensable advice has helped me to write an even better book.

GENOGRAM

To the best of your ability, complete the following genogram. The genogram may help you identify racial trauma passed down to you from your ancestors. If you have gaps in knowledge, you may need to get an oral history from family members. On or next to each symbol list the name, birth date, and death date of the family member, and any significant traits, illness, trauma, dysfunction, and blessings of God. Insert a symbol for each additional family member. If you want to go farther back in your family line, simply add to the top of the genogram. Your genogram may reveal the need for prayer and counseling for uncovered wounds as well as blessings.

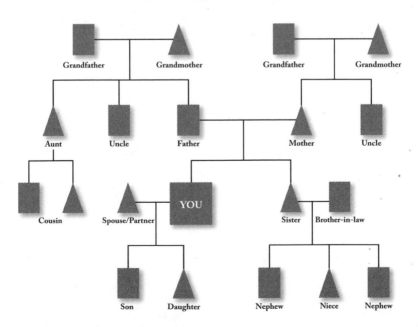

GROUP DISCUSSION GUIDE

This guide offers an opportunity for greater reflection, discussion, and prayer in a small-group setting. The small group may consist of a few friends or members of a church or community. However, it's essential to use a great deal of care when choosing who should participate in the group and how to engage in group discussions. The topic of racial trauma can stir up a deep well of emotions for people of color, and echoes of their own trauma for White folks. To allow for deep conversation and processing of the material, the group must be a safe place for everyone.

The following are some suggestions to make it safer.

There should be a group facilitator to direct conversation, handle conflicts, pray, and be available for follow-up. The facilitator also should watch for any members who are having a difficult time emotionally and may need to obtain more outside support.

Have group members help set ground rules and agree to these and any predetermined ones such as a full commitment to confidentiality. What is said in the group stays in the group.

Group members must have a listen-and-learn posture that respects experiences that are different from their own. This is especially needed if the group is racially mixed.

If you are concerned that people will not feel safe and comfortable to share freely, consider having a group that is exclusively for people of color or for White folks.

In this guide, the ten chapters of the book are divided among four sessions. Group members should read the chapters and complete the questions before each group meeting. They should come to the group prepared to share how the chapters affected them and to discuss any broader implications. The discussions should prompt group members to pray for themselves outside the group and to pray for one another in the group. I hope these discussions will encourage and strengthen the faith of group members, help in the journey of healing racial trauma, and spur the members on to good works to combat racism and racial trauma.

MEETING 1

The objective of this first meeting is for group members to get acclimated and to engage the discussion questions. Start by setting the ground rules. Then have the members take a couple of minutes each to share who they are and one important thing they want to share about their racial and ethnic background. Then proceed to process the chapter questions.

Chapter 1: Wounds

1. Discuss how Jeremiah 6:14 (see the epigraph) relates to racial trauma in the lives of people of color.

2. In this chapter, are there experiences of racism or racial trauma that you can relate to?

3. Can you share with the group any generational trauma or blessings of God from past generations that were revealed in the genogram you completed?

4. Pray for one another and listen for how you may be carrying symptoms of racial trauma.

Chapter 2: Fatigue

1. How have you experienced racial battle fatigue like a yoke (see Lamentations 5:5 in the epigraph)?

2. What kind of support do you need right now within and outside of the group?

3. Pray and release your battle fatigue to the Lord. Exchange any burden you carry for his lighter burden and greater strength.

Chapter 3: Silence

1. How have you been silenced in your life?

2. What can you do now to reclaim your voice?

3. What can you do to accept and care for your mind and body?

4. Pray for physical and emotional healing.

MEETING 2

The objective of this meeting is to discuss the impact of rage and fear in your lives. As strong feelings surface, it's essential to be present with the members and to end each section in prayer.

Chapter 4: Rage

1. Discuss what you think is the meaning of the African proverb in this chapter's epigraph.

2. Are you struggling with anger and rage? If so, why and how is it expressed?

3. What are some things that can help you to process your anger or rage?

4. How is the Lord calling you to harness your anger for your benefit and that of others?

Chapter 5: Fear

1. How have fear and anxiety affected your life?

2. What kind of support or activity do you think will help when your fear or anxiety is triggered?

3. Ask the Lord for his perfect love to cast out fear and to fill you with peace.

MEETING 3

The objective of meeting three is to examine the importance of lament and the way that shame and addiction have hampered healing and resilience.

Chapter 6: Lament

1. Can you relate to C. S. Lewis's sentiment about grief in the epigraph to chapter six? Explain.

2. Can you be honest with God and share your full range of feelings with him? Why or why not?

3. Write out a prayer of lament to God and share it in the group.

4. In prayer ask the Lord for his comfort through Scripture, words, or images that assure you of his presence.

Chapter 7: Shame

1. Has the Lord revealed to you any hidden shame? If so, what are the sources?

2. Are you ready to lay down your shame? If so, how would this change you, your life, or that of others?

3. How have people in your life shamed you?

4. How do you diminish or shame yourself for not "measuring up"?

Chapter 8: Addiction

5. Identify your triggers. "I know that I am most likely in a cycle when the following happens."

6. Write out the thoughts you think to convince yourself that acting out is all right.

7. What truths do you know that can counter these thoughts?

8. What specific actions can you take when you become aware that you are being triggered, preoccupied with addictive thoughts and issues, or tempted?

MEETING 4

The objective of the final meeting is to help members carefully look at the process of healing racial trauma and becoming more resilient in the future. Members should share what has been helpful to them on this healing journey. The group might decide to express their faith by engaging in some form of collective social justice action. The group should end with a prayer for each member, the community, the church, and the world.

Chapter 9: Freedom

1. Write down all the ways that God has directly or indirectly met your needs.

2. Are your gifts or abilities locked up because of racial trauma? Write a prayer about what you want to reclaim. Then ask God how to do it.

3. We are forgiven. Now we are to forgive. Take a couple of deep breaths and sit silently and listen. Identify someone you need to forgive and get him or her clearly in mind. Take a sheet of paper and write that person's name at the top. Now ask yourself if you are willing to forgive this person totally, absolutely, and

unconditionally. If so, in prayer as you hand the person over to God, say, "I forgive you and release you to Jesus."

Chapter 10: Resilience

1. How can you grow in resilience?

2. Write and share your soul care plan.

3. How will you drive a spoke into the wheels of injustice?

4. How can you engage in activism?

GLOSSARY

addiction: When the pain of racial trauma becomes unbearable, we want to numb ourselves, so we use our addictive behavior to help us to function and carry on with our lives.

apartheid: The brutal, racist, segregationist policy of the minority White population that disempowered Black South Africans.

bitter root: Deeply held unforgiveness and bitterness because of past hurts.

breakaway guilt: A phenomenon occurring when people of color decide to attend and graduate from college. They feel guilty because they fear it will disconnect them from their family and community.

burnout: When work becomes overwhelming and seemingly impossible.

Christ-centered care: When the care, prayer, and support that a person receives is biblically grounded and centered in the complete work of Jesus Christ that brings hope and healing.

code-switching: When people of color change how they speak or behave so they are more aligned and acceptable to the dominant White culture.

colorism: When people of the same ethnic or racial group harbor internalized racism and engage in prejudice or discrimination against individuals with a dark skin tone.

compounded grief: Several "unpredictable and uncontrollable" losses, each capable of producing extreme stress and decreased physical, psychological, and relational health.

cycle of revenge: The belief that relief from pain can only occur if its source or cause is punished or destroyed.

defensive othering: When a person attempts to join the dominant group by sharing the same attitudes and disdain toward coethnics.

Deferred Action for Childhood Arrivals (DACA): A program that granted temporary resident status for those who were illegally brought into the country as children, who are often referred to as Dreamers.

double consciousness: The sense that people of color are "always looking at one's own self through the eyes of others, of measuring one's soul by the tape of a world that looks on in amused contempt and pity." (quote by W. E. B. Du Bois)

environmental racism: A collective form of racism in which poor communities are disproportionately exposed to air, water, and chemical pollutants and are denied the same high-quality municipal services that White communities receive.

fight: Being combative for good or bad, which may or may not involve violence.

flee: Denying, minimizing, ignoring, or laughing off racism as if it doesn't matter.

fold: Harboring self-doubt and questioning whether one belongs, is accepted, or is acceptable.

forfeit: Denying who one is and what one wants and needs.

forgiveness: Forgiveness involves letting go of our desire for revenge. This frees us to move on in life regardless of what the perpetrator did or does.

healing-centered engagement: Changing the focus from "what's wrong with you" to "what's right with you."

historical racial trauma: Trauma shared by a group rather than an individual; it often spans multiple generations.

impostor phenomenon (or syndrome): When high achievers of color are unable to internalize and accept their success, fearing that others will eventually unmask them as a fraud.

internalize racism: When people think and act negatively toward themselves and others in their communities. They collude with personal and systemic racism that reinforces the power and privilege of White people and undermines the authority of people of color.

internalized racism: Relishing a role as the exception, yet underneath the façade lies self-hatred that sides with the oppressor and gives tacit approval to the tools of oppression.

interpersonal racism: A person demeaning and degrading the gifts, calling, motives, and body of a person of color.

John Henryism Scale: A scale used to identify those who have physically suffered as a result of their constant and excessive striving or work.

lament: An honest form of prayer in which we weep, complain, scream, or wrestle with God over the pain or injustice we see or experience.

listening prayer: In prayer, a person listens with or without another person for a sense of clarity from the Lord. Jesus modeled this two-way communication with God the Father. Used in counseling it has helped people allow God to uncover trauma and administer healing.

microaggressions: Minor racist hassles, a large number of which can add up and wear down a person, making them vulnerable to poor health.

model minority: Minority group seen as a model for other minorities because it is depicted as noncomplaining, not attracting negative attention, and not causing problems.

moral injury: Participating in, witnessing, or failing to prevent acts that transgress deeply held moral beliefs and expectations.

personal racial trauma: When a person directly experiences racism that results in racial trauma.

physical racial trauma: Racially motivated physical violence.

post-traumatic growth (PTG): Resilience and growth that can occur following a traumatic event; the individual derives meaning from an incident that caused suffering.

powwow: A gathering of First Nation tribes dressed in indigenous attire and performing traditional drumming and dancing while outsiders observe; also a time for tribes to unite and strategize.

public space racism: When racial terror symbols are used in a public space (e.g., a burning cross in a field); this metacommunication sparks a conversation about who is dominant, worthy, and belongs.

racial battle fatigue: Mental and physical stress and weariness people of color face from racism; it is similar to what a soldier experiences in battle.

racial gaslighting: Manipulating or questioning a person of color's sense of reality, often to assert or maintain control, superiority, or power.

racial profiling: When people of color are considered suspect and are stopped by the police without cause.

rehumanizing: Acknowledging the pain felt by those on the opposite side of a conflict; this may allow the victim to gradually develop compassion toward the perpetrator.

repair: Addressing and rectifying systemic injustice on a micro- or macrolevel.

resilience: The ability to face, learn from, and grow stronger from life's challenges.

Shinnecock: A First Nation people and reservation on the southeastern edge of Long Island, south of Great Peconic Bay. In English, Shinnecock means "people of the stony shore."

soul care: Resting, destressing, exposing injustice, and advocating for one's own needs and those of others.

soul repair: The process of healing from a moral injury such as racial trauma.

spatial racism: Dominance is communicated when spaces and structures are purposefully designed to divide or change the demographics of communities.

stereotype threat: The unconscious fear of living up to a negative stereotype about one's own group. Instead of trying to prevent this, the person self-sabotages, which ironically causes him or her to live up to the feared stereotype.

stop and frisk: When people of color are considered suspect without cause and are stopped by the police and patted down in a search for contraband.

systemic racism: Black activist Stokely Carmichael coined *institutional racism* as "the collective failure of an organization to provide an appropriate and professional service to people because of their color, culture or ethnic origin."

transgenerational racial trauma: The experience of trauma transmitted across a specific family line.

trauma-informed care: When everyone has experienced some level of trauma, everyone is treated in a way that promotes safety, empowerment, and healing.

true reconciliation: Occurs when a perpetrator personally and publicly apologizes for past and present harm. Also must include a commitment to stop all actions of injustice and oppression, and repair any damage done.

Truth and Reconciliation Commission (TRC): Established in South Africa to provide an opportunity for victims and perpetrators under apartheid to tell the truth and give and receive apologies; many perpetrators received amnesty for their crimes.

vicarious trauma: The trauma that results after one sees or hears the secondhand, detailed trauma stories of the deceased or survivors.

White privilege: The acts of entitlement and unmerited benefit that White people receive, unconsciously or consciously.

woke: When a person is aware of the history and current reality of racism, White supremacy, systemic oppression, and injustice in the United States and around the world.

NOTES

1 WOUNDS

[1]"The Forgotten Riot That Sparked Boston's Racial Unrest," *Boston Globe*, June 2, 2017, www.boston.com/news/local-news/2017/06/02/the-forgotten -riot-that-sparked-bostons-racial-unrest.

[2]Martin Luther King Jr., "The Other America," Grosse Pointe Historical Society, accessed May 9, 2019, www.gphistorical.org/mlk/mlkspeech. This speech was delivered March 14, 1968, at Grosse Pointe High School, MI.

[3]Monnica Williams, "Can Racism Cause PTSD? Implications for DSM-5," *Psychology Today*, May 20, 2013, www.psychologytoday.com/us/blog /culturally-speaking/201305/can-racism-cause-ptsd-implications-dsm-5.

[4]Danice L. Brown, and Tracy L. Tylka, "Racial Discrimination and Resilience in African American Young Adults: Examining Racial Socialization as a Moderator," *Journal of Black Psychology* 37, no. 3 (2010): https://doi.org /10.1177/0095798410390689.

[5]Martin Luther King Jr., "I've Been to the Mountaintop," *AFSCME*, accessed July 1, 2019, https://m.afscme.org/union/history/mlk/ive-been-to-the -mountaintop-by-dr-martin-luther-king-jr. This speech was delivered April 3, 1968, at the Mason Temple, Memphis, TN.

[6]William Macpherson of Cluny, "The Stephen Lawrence Inquiry," February 1999, 6.34, https://assets.publishing.service.gov.uk/government /uploads/system/...data/.../4262.pdf. This quote is also attributed to 1960's Black activist Stokely Carmichael.

[7]Karen D. Pyke, "What Is Internalized Racial Oppression and Why Don't We Study it? Acknowledging Racism's Hidden Injuries," *Sociological Perspectives* 53, no. 4 (winter 2010): 551-72.

[8]Robert T. Carter, "Racism and Psychological and Emotional Injury: Recognizing and Assessing Race-based Traumatic Stress," *Counseling Psychologist* 35, no. 1 (2007): 13-105.

[9]Walter Howard Smith Jr., "The Impact of Racial Trauma on African Americans," Heinz Endowments, February 16, 2010, www.heinz.org /userfiles/impactofracialtraumaonafricanamericans.pdf.

[10]Vincent Mobatt, Azure B. Thompson, Nghi D. Thai, and Jacob Kraemer, "Historical Trauma as Public Narrative: A Conceptual Review of How History Impacts Present-day Health," *Social Science & Medicine* 106 (April 2014): 128-36.

[11]Ann Piccard, "Death by Boarding School: 'The Last Acceptable Racism' and the United States' Genocide of Native Americans," *Gonzaga Law Review* 49, no. 1 (December 2013): 161.

[12]Satsuki Ina, "Tule Lake Reunion Symposium," Children of the Camps Project, June 1998, www.pbs.org/childofcamp/project/remarks.html.

[13]Barri Belnap, "Turns of a Phrase: Traumatic Learning Through the Generations," in *Lost in Transmission: Studies of Trauma Across Generations*, ed. M. Gerard Fromm (New York: Routledge, 2018), chap.7.

[14]Carter, "Racism and Psychological and Emotional Injury," 26.

[15]Thema Bryant-Davis and Carlota Ocampo, "The Trauma of Racism: Implications for Counseling, Research, and Education," *The Counseling Psychologist* 33, no. 4 (July 2005): 574.

[16]Joseph McDonald, introduction to *Exploring Moral Injury in Sacred Texts*, ed. Joseph McDonald (London: Jessica Kingsley, 2017), 17.

[17]Rita Nakashima Brock, foreword to *Exploring Moral Injury*, 9.

2 FATIGUE

[1]Hannah Walker, "Unspoken Immunity and Reimagined Justice: The Potential for Implementing Restorative Justice and Community Justice Models in Police-related Shootings," *PACE Law Review* 37, no. 2 (spring 2017): art. 10.

[2]Phillip Atiba Goff et al., "The Essence of Innocence: Consequences of Dehumanizing Black Children," *Journal of Personality and Social Psychology* 106, no. 4 (2014): 526.

[3]David Love, "'Racial Battle Fatigue' Is Real: Victims of Racial Micro-aggressions Are Stressed Like Soldiers in War," *Atlantic Black Star*, November 11, 2016, https://atlantablackstar.com/2016/11/11/racial-battle

-fatigue-is-real-victims-of-racial-microaggressions-are-stressed-like
-soldiers-in-war.

[4]"Fatigue," Mayo Clinic, January 11, 2018, www.mayoclinic.org/symptoms
/fatigue/basics/definition/sym-20050894.

[5]Paul C. Gorski, "Fighting Racism, Battling Burnout: Causes of Activist
Burnout in US Racial Justice Activists," *Ethnic and Racial Studies* 42, no. 5
(Feb. 2018): 667-87.

[6]Martin Luther King, "Martin Luther King Jr. in Boston," *Boston Globe*,
April 22, 1965, www3.bostonglobe.com/specials/insiders/2013/01/16/martin
-luther-king-boston/Dl3u3m2yzuTyGnM1xh5BhM/picture.html?
arc404=true. Dr. King gave this speech at demonstration at the Patrick T.
Campbell Middle School in Roxbury, MA.

[7]Martin Luther King Jr., "Sermon at Temple Israel of Hollywood," *American
Rhetoric*, February 26, 1965, https://americanrhetoric.com/speeches/mlk
templeisraelhollywood.htm.

[8]Bruce Gellerman, "'It Was Like a War Zone': Busing in Boston," *Earthwhile*,
September 5, 2014, www.wbur.org/news/2014/09/05/boston-busing
-anniversary.

[9]Linda Banks-Santilli, "First-Generation College Students and Their Pursuit
of the American Dream," *Journal of Case Studies in Education* 5 (February 2014):
1-35.

[10]Claude M. Steele and J. Aronson, "Stereotype Threat and Intellectual Test
Performance of African Americans," *Journal of Personality and Social
Psychology* 69, no. 5 (1995): 797-811.

[11]Howard B. London, "Breaking Away: A Study of First-Generation College
Students and Their Families," *American Journal of Education* 9, no. 2
(February 1989): 144-70.

3 SILENCE

[1]Lawson Fusao Inada, ed., *Only What We Could Carry: The Japanese American
Internment Experience* (Berkeley, CA: Heyday Books, 2000).

[2]Floyd Schmoe, quoted in Stephanie Bangarth, "Religious Organizations
and the 'Relocation' of Persons of Japanese Ancestry in North America:
Evaluating Advocacy," *American Review of Canadian Studies* (autumn 2004):
511-40.

[3]Jeff Guo, "Before People Start Invoking Japanese American Internment,
They Should Remember What It Was Like," *Washington Post*, November 18,
2015, www.washingtonpost.com/news/wonk/wp/2015/11/18/before-people

-start-invoking-japanese-american-internment-they-should-remember
-what-it-was-like/?utm_term=.6145c02410d7.

[4]Michi Weglyn, *Years of Infamy: the Untold Story of America's Concentration Camps* (New York: William Morrow, 1976), 312.

[5]Satsuki Ina, "Tule Lake Reunion Symposium," Children of the Camps Project, June 1998, www.pbs.org/childofcamp/project/remarks.html.

[6]Gwendolyn M. Jensen, *The Experience of Injustice: Health Consequences of the Japanese American Internment* (dissertation, University of Colorado, 1997).

[7]A. K. Staggers, "'I Can't Breathe': African-Americans, Race Trauma and PTSD," *Atlanta Black Star,* September 6, 2015, https://atlantablackstar .com/2015/09/06/cant-breathe-african-americans-race-trauma-ptsd.

[8]Maya Salam, "For Serena Williams, Childbirth Was a Harrowing Ordeal. She's Not Alone," *New York Times,* November 1, 2011, www.nytimes.com /2018/01/11/sports/tennis/serena-williams-baby-vogue.html.

[9]Bessel van der Kolk, *The Body Keeps the Score: Brain, Mind, and Body in the Healing of Trauma* (New York: Penguin Books, 2014), 2.

[10]James Hamblin, "Why Succeeding Against the Odds Can Make You Sick," *New York Times,* January 27, 2017, www.nytimes.com/2017/01/27/opinion /sunday/why-succeeding-against-the-odds-can-make-you-sick.html.

[11]Elie Wiesel, "Nobel Prize Acceptance Speech," December 10, 1986, Oslo, Norway, http://eliewieselfoundation.org/elie-wiesel/nobelprizespeech.

[12]Nobu Miyoshi, "Identity Crisis of the Sansei and the Concentration Camp," Legacy of Camps, San Francisco, May 13-15, 1998, www.momomedia.com /CLPEF/sansei/identity.htm.

[13]van der Kolk, *Body Keeps the Score,* 235.

[14]Adia Harvey Wingfield, "The Professional Burdens of Being a 'Model Minority,'" *Atlantic,* June 6, 2016, www.theatlantic.com/business/archive /2016/06/professional-burdens-model-minority-asian-americans/485492.

[15]Jeff Guo, "The Real Secret to Asian American Success Was Not Education" *Washington Post,* November 19, 2016, www.washingtonpost.com/news /wonk/wp/2016/11/19/the-real-secret-to-asian-american-success-was -not-education.

[16]Chhaya Chhoum, executive director of Mekong NYC, in Kimberly Yam, "Asian-Americans Have Highest Poverty Rate In NYC, but Stereotypes Make the Issue Invisible," *Huffington Post,* May 8, 2017, www.huffington post.com/entry/asian-american-poverty-nyc_us_58ff7f40e4b0c46f0782a5b6.

[17]Wingfield, "Professional Burdens of Being a 'Model Minority.'"

[18]Donna K. Nagata, *Legacy of Injustice: Exploring the Cross-Generational Impact of the Japanese American Internment* (New York: Plenum Press, 1993), 95.

[19]Donna K. Nagata, "Psychological Effects of Camp," *Densho Encyclopedia*, accessed November 2, 2018, http://encyclopedia.densho.org/Psychological_effects_of_camp.

[20]Kristen Cooksey-Stowers et al., "Food Swamps Predict Obesity Rates Better Than Food Deserts in the United States," *International Journal of Environmental Research and Public Health*. 14, no. 11 (2017): 1366, www.ncbi.nlm.nih.gov/pmc/articles/PMC5708005.

4 RAGE

[1]Na'im Akbar, *Chains and Images of Psychological Slavery* (Jersey City, NJ: New Mind Productions, 1996), 31.

[2]Michelle Alexander, *The New Jim Crow: Mass Incarceration in the Age of Colorblindness* (New York: New Press, 2012), 247.

[3]Kenneth V. Hardy, "Healing the Hidden Wounds of Racial Trauma," *Reclaiming Children and Youth* 22, no. 1 (spring 2013): 26.

[4]Lisa V. Blitz, Mary Pender Greene, "Racism and Racial Identity: Reflections on Urban Practice in Mental Health," *Journal of Emotional Abuse*, 6, no. 2/3 (2006): 20.

[5]Ralph Ellison, *Invisible Man* (New York: Random House, 1952), 3.

[6]Michell Nunez and Madeline Wordes, "Our Vulnerable Teenagers: Their Victimization, Its Consequences, and Directions for Prevention and Intervention," National Center for the Victims of Crime, May 2002, https://victimsofcrime.org/docs/Documents/teen_victim_report.pdf.

[7]Dexter R. Voisin, "The Effects of Family and Community Violence Exposure Among Youth: Recommendations for Practice and Policy," *Journal of Social Work Education* 43, no. 1 (winter 2007): 51-66.

[8]"Stop and Frisk—The Human Impact," Center for Constitutional Rights, July 2012, https://ccrjustice.org/sites/default/files/attach/2015/08/the-human-impact-report.pdf.

[9]Alexander, *The New Jim Crow*, 261.

[10]Janet Currie and Erdal Tekin, "Does Child Abuse Cause Crime?" National Bureau of Economic Research, April 2006, 27-28.

[11]Hardy, "Healing the Hidden Wounds of Racial Trauma," 28.

5 FEAR

[1]Bryan Stevenson, "Lynching in America: Confronting the Legacy of Racial Terror," 3rd ed., Equal Justice Initiative, 2017, https://lynchinginamerica.eji .org/report.

[2]Francis Jennings, *The Invasion of America: Indians, Colonialism and the Cant of Conquest* (New York: Norton, 1976).

[3]Shinnecock Indian Nation v. State of New York, 05-CV-2887 (TCP) (US District Court, E.D. New York Nov. 28, 2006), id.10, https://sct.narf.org /documents/shinnecock_v_ny_15-1215/cert_petition.pdf.

[4]Peggy Spellman Hoey, "Shinnecock Protests 'Stolen Land,'" *Independent,* June 12, 2018, https://indyeastend.com/news-opinion/south-fork /shinnecock-protests-stolen-land.

[5]Michael S. Schmidt and Eric Lichtblau, "Racial Profiling Rife at Airport, U.S. Officers Say," *New York Times,* August 11, 2012, www.nytimes.com/2012 /08/12/us/racial-profiling-at-boston-airport-officials-say.html.

[6]Maya Angelou, "Maya Angelou Quotes," *AZ Quotes,* May 1, 2014, www .azquotes.com/quote/1158328.

[7]Morgan Lee, "A Deeper Debate Over Drums in Church," *Christianity Today* August 18, 2017, www.christianitytoday.com/ct/2017/september /native-american-worship-drums-in-church-debate.html.

[8]Deborah Pardo-Kaplan, "Jesus, the Frybread of Life," *Christianity Today,* May 15, 2017, www.christianitytoday.com/women/2017/may/jesus-frybread -of-life.html.

[9]Lisa Finn, "Town Buys Shinnecock Burial Ground Where Human Remains Were Found," *Patch* (Southampton), February 7, 2019 https://patch.com /new-york/southampton/town-buys-shinnecock-burial-ground-where -human-remains-were-found.

[10]Audre Lorde, *A Burst of Light* (Mineola, NY: Courier Dover, 2017), 130.

6 LAMENT

[1]"Listen to a Distraught Guatemalan Child Call His Mother from a U.S. Immigration Shelter," *Vice News,* June 28, 2018, www.youtube.com/watch ?v=RQRnp8U9AJw.

[2]Soong-Chan Rah, *Prophetic Lament: A Call for Justice in Troubled Times* (Downers Grove, IL: InterVarsity Press, 2015), 44.

[3]Emmanuel Katongole, quoted in Bruce Fields, "When He Died Upon the Tree," *Christianity Today*, August 16, 2017, www.christianitytoday.com /ct/2017/august-web-only/reflections-on-cross-and-lynching-tree.html.

[4]Glen Schiraldi, *The Post-Traumatic Stress Disorder Sourcebook* (New York: McGraw Hill, 2000), 237.

[5]Mimi Abramovitz and Jochen Albrecht, quoted in Dottie Lebron et al., "The Trauma of Racism," McSilver Institute for Poverty Policy and Research, 2015, 20, mcsilver.nyu.edu/sites/default/files/reports/Trauma-of-Racism-Report.pdf.

[6]Lebron, "Trauma of Racism," 21.

[7]Carrie Hemmings and Amanda M. Evans, "Identifying and Treating Race-Based Trauma in Counseling," *Journal of Multicultural Counseling and Development* 46, no. 1 (2018), 20-39.

[8]Schiraldi, *Post-Traumatic Stress Disorder Sourcebook*, 241-42.

[9]Christie Renick, "Translating Trauma Therapy for Hispanic and Latino Communities," *Chronicle of Social Change,* May 18, 2018, https://chronicleof socialchange.org/news-2/adapting-trauma-therapy-hispanic-latino -communities.

[10]Susana Rivera, quoted in Renick, "Translating Trauma Therapy."

[11]"Discrimination in America: Experiences and Views of Latinos," *National Public Radio,* October 2017, 26, www.npr.org/documents/2017/oct/discrimination -latinos-final.pdf.

[12]D. Kaminer, D. J. Stein, I. Mbanga, N. Zungu-Dirwayi, "The Truth and Reconciliation Commission in South Africa," *British Journal of Psychiatry* 178, no. 4 (2001): 373-77.

[13]Susanna Harper, *The Psychological Impact of Apartheid on Black South Africans* (Freiburg, Germany: University of Education Freiburg, 2012).

[14]Rah, *Prophetic Lament*, 47.

[15]John E. Welshons, *Awakening from Grief* (Little Falls, NJ: Open Heart Publications, 2002), 159.

[16]Rah, *Prophetic Lament*, 59.

7 SHAME

[1]Karen Tumulty, "Wife Killing Puts Boston in Worst Racial Crisis in Years," *Los Angeles Times,* January 10, 1990, 1.

[2]Brené Brown, *I Thought It Was Just Me (But It Isn't): Making the Journey from "What Will People Think?" to "I Am Enough"* (New York: Gotham Books, 2008), xxv.

[3]Kirsten Weir, "Feel Like a Fraud?" *gradPSYCH* 11, no. 4 (November 2013), 24.

[4]G. Di Pietro et al., "Racial Differences in the Diagnosis and Treatment of Prostate Cancer," *International Neurology Journal* 20, no. s2 (November 2016): S112-19.

[5]W. E. B. Du Bois, *The Souls of Black Folk* (1904; repr. Chicago: A. C. McClurg, 1989), 41.

8 ADDICTION

[1]Bryan Holland, "Mildred and Richard: The Love Story That Changed America," *History.com*, February 17, 2017, www.history.com/news/mildred -and-richard-the-love-story-that-changed-america.

[2]Loving v. Virginia, 388 U.S. 1 (1967). Excerpts from a transcript of oral arguments on April 10, 1967.

[3]Saera Khan, "Confronting Complex Multiracial Realities: The Daily Life of Multiracial Americans," *Psychology Today*, June 1, 2017, www.psychology today.com/us/blog/unseen-and-unheard/201706/confronting-complex -multiracial-realities.

[4]Khan, "Confronting Complex Multiracial Realities."

[5]Tim Stoddart, "Addiction—Cunning, Baffling and Powerful," *SoberNation*, August 26, 2013, https://sobernation.com/cunning-baffling-and-powerful.

[6]Khan, "Confronting Complex Multiracial Realities."

[7]Khan, "Confronting Complex Multiracial Realities."

[8]"Multiracial in America: Proud, Diverse and Growing in Numbers," Pew Research Center, June 11, 2015, www.pewsocialtrends.org/2015/06/11 /multiracial-in-america.

[9]Khan, "Confronting Complex Multiracial Realities."

9 FREEDOM

[1]Shawn Ginwright, "The Future of Healing: Shifting from Trauma Informed Care to Healing Centered Engagement," *Medium.com*, May 31, 2018, https://medium.com/@ginwright/the-future-of-healing-shifting-from -trauma-informed-care-to-healing-centered-engagement-634f557ce69c.

[2]Cardwell C. Nuckols, "Treating Moral Injury," National Association for Addiction Professionals, accessed May 30, 2019, www.naadac.org/assets /2416/cardwell_nuckols_treatingmoral.pdf.

[3]C. D. Campbell and T. Evans-Campbell, "Historical Trauma and Native American Child Development and Mental Health: An Overview," in *American Indian and Alaska Native Children and Mental Health: Development, Context, Prevention, and Treatment*, ed. M. Sarche, P. Spicer, P. Farrell, H. E. Fitzgerald (Santa Barbara, CA: Praeger, 2011), 1-26. See also Vincent Mobatt et al., *Historical Trauma as Public Narrative: A Conceptual Review of How History Impacts Present-Day Health, Social Science and Medicine* 106 (April 2014): 128-36.

[4]Isabelle Mansuy and Erika Beras, "Traces of Genetic Trauma Can Be Tweaked," *Scientific American*, April 15, 2017, www.scientificamerican.com /podcast/episode/traces-of-genetic-trauma-can-be-tweaked/?redirect=1.

[5]J. Rappaport and R. Simkins, "Healing and Empowering Through Community Narrative," *Prevention in Human Services* 10, no. 1 (1991): 29-50.

[6]A. R. Denham, "Rethinking Historical Trauma: Narratives of Resilience," *Transcultural Psychiatry* 45, no. 3 (2008): 391-414.

[7]Olga Botcharova, "Implementation of Track Two Diplomacy: Developing a Model of Forgiveness," in *Forgiveness and Reconciliation: Religion, Public Policy and Conflict Transformation*, ed. Raymond G. Helmick and Rodney L. Petersen (West Conshohocken, PA: Templeton Foundation Press, 2001), 291-92.

[8]Botcharova, "Implementation of Track Two Diplomacy," 293.

[9]Claudia Black, *Changing Course*, 2nd ed. (Center City, MN: Hazelden Publishing, 2002), 213.

[10]Amanda M. Evans, "Responding to Race-Related Trauma: Counseling and Research Recommendations to Promote Post Traumatic Growth when Counseling African American Males," *Journal of Counselor Preparation and Supervision* 8, no.1 (2016): 8.

[11]Botcharova, "Implementation of Track Two Diplomacy," 293.

[12]Bruce Gellerman, "Busing Left Deep Scars on Boston, Its Students," *WBUR*, September 5, 2014, www.wbur.org/news/2014/09/05/boston -busing-effects.

[13]Martin Luther King Jr., *I Have A Dream . . .*" National Archives, August 28, 1963, www.archives.gov/files/press/exhibits/dream-speech.pdf.

[14]Miroslav Volf, *Exclusion and Embrace* (Nashville: Abingdon Press, 1996).

10 RESILIENCE

[1]Lena Horne, quoted in "Lena Horne," *BluegrassSpecial.com*, June 2010, www .thebluegrassspecial.com/archive/2010/june10/lena-horne-obit.php.

[2]James H. Cone, *The Cross and the Lynching Tree* (Maryknoll, NY: Orbis, 2011), 18.

[3]D. Watts-Jones, "Healing Internalized Racism: The Role of a Within-Group Sanctuary Among People of African Descent," *Family Process* no. 4 (2002), 41.

[4]Frederick Buechner, *Wishful Thinking* (New York: Harper & Row 1973), 53-54.

[5]Dietrich Bonhoeffer, "The Church and the Jewish Question," in *A Testament to Freedom: The Essential Writings of Dietrich Bonhoeffer*, ed. Geffrey B. Kelly and F. Burton Nelson (New York: HarperCollins, 1995), 130-33.

[6]Katie Couric, "The Blood of Lynching Victims Is in the Soil," *National Geographic Magazine*, April 2018, 150.